A SATIE CLARINET ALBUM

arranged by Sidney Lawton

Novello

CONTENTS

Foreword

This album of arrangements of some of the piano works of Erik Satie (1866 – 1925) has been based on the edition compiled and edited from the original printed copies by Peter Dickinson and Desmond Ratcliffe (Novello, 1976).

Players are recommended to read Peter Dickinson's introduction to that edition, which contains much useful and interesting information on Satie and his style.

In this edition, whilst faithfully preserving every musical essential of the originals, it has been found necessary to transpose most of the keys to suit the fingering of the B flat clarinet. Also, in order that the players should be able to keep in touch, in the *Trois Gnossiennes*, I have added obvious time-signatures and barlines. It is hoped that this edition will assist clarinettists by making a wider range of Satie's music available to them than exists at present.

S.L.

A SATIE CLARINET ALBUM

Arranged by
SIDNEY LAWTON

1 JE TE VEUX - VALSE

(composed 1903 - 1904)

retenir   très
retenu

a tempo

retenir

très
retenu

a tempo

retenir

très
retenu

a tempo

2 POUDRE D'OR - VALSE

(composed 1900)

14

* small notes as an alternative

3 LE PICCADILLY - MARCHE

(composed 1900)

Pas trop vite

TRIO

4 TROIS GYMNOPÉDIES

(composed 1888)

I

Lent et douloureux

II

Lent et triste

III

5 TROIS GNOSSIENNES
(composed 1890)

I

II

(Lent)

III

Lent

The NYPD: The History and Legacy of the New York City

By Charles River Editors

About Charles River Editors

Charles River Editors is a boutique digital publishing company, specializing in bringing history back to life with educational and engaging books on a wide range of topics. Keep up to date with our new and free offerings with this 5 second sign up on our weekly mailing list, and visit Our Kindle Author Page to see other recently published Kindle titles.

We make these books for you and always want to know our readers' opinions, so we encourage you to leave reviews and look forward to publishing new and exciting titles each week.

Introduction

"I would give the greatest sunset in the world for one sight of New York's skyline. The shapes and the thought that made them. The sky over New York and the will of man made visible... Let them come to New York, stand on the shore of the Hudson, look and kneel. When I see the city from my window - no, I don't feel how small I am - but I feel that if a war came to threaten this, I would like to throw myself into space, over the city, and protect these buildings with my body."
– Ayn Rand, The Fountainhead

Of all the great cities in the world, few personify their country like New York City. As America's largest city and best known immigration gateway into the country, NYC represents the beauty, diversity and sheer strength of the United States, a global financial center that has enticed people chasing the "American Dream" for centuries.

America's prototypical metropolis was once a serene landscape in which Native American tribes farmed and fished, but when European settlers arrived its location on the Eastern seaboard sparked a rapid transformation. Given its history of rapid change, it is ironic that the city's inhabitants often complain about the city's changing and yearn for things to stay the same. The website EV Grieve, whose name plays on the idea that the East Village "grieves" for the history and character the neighborhood loses every day to market forces and gentrification, regularly features a photo of some site, usually of little interest: an abandoned store, a small bodega, a vacant lot. The caption says, simply, that this is what the site looked like on a given day. The editors of the website are determined to document everything and anything for future generations.

That is hardly a modern phenomenon. New Yorkers have always grieved over the city's continuous upheavals and ever-increasing size and complexity. By the 1820s, Wall Street had lost whatever charm it might have had; former residents complained that two-story houses had given way to intimidating five-story office buildings. The New York Commercial Advertiser noted in 1825 that "Greenwich is no longer a country village," but rather an up-and-coming neighborhood. Today, it's hard to find a history of New York City that doesn't refer to Henry James's famous 1908 story The Jolly Corner, in which a man returns to New York after decades abroad only to be horrified by an unfamiliar hellscape of commercial growth. He finds his once-jolly childhood home nearly buried "among the dreadful multiplied numberings which seemed to him to reduce the whole place to some vast ledger-page, overgrown, fantastic, of ruled and criss-crossed lines and figures." The once-beloved city has transformed itself into "the mere gross generalisation of wealth and force and success." That childhood home—an 1830s townhouse—in fact belonged to the James family on Washington Square in Greenwich Village. It was destroyed to make way for New York University, which is today embroiled in yet another real estate saga as it plans to expand once again.

While America's biggest city constantly changes, the largest police force in the United States, the New York Police Department, is no stranger to the limelight. Quite the contrary, the NYPD has become immutably entrenched in American culture, past and present. The acronym itself, while a mouthful, is effortlessly musical and therefore commands a certain presence. It is also the most internationally renowned police department, recognizable even to non-Americans and non-native English speakers, thanks to the virtually incalculable depictions of the department in various forms of literature, movies, and television shows. Chances are people across the world have stumbled on media depictions of the NYPD, such as Sidney Lumet's *Serpico*, the *Die Hard* franchise, *NYPD Blue*, and even lighthearted comedies like *Brooklyn Nine-Nine*.

Of course, the limelight is much like a double-edged sword, and there is a noticeable rift in New Yorkers' perception of their homegrown police force. To some, NYPD officers – excluding a few bad eggs – have, throughout history, endeavored above and beyond time and again to fulfill their duty to protect and serve. Their valiance is best exemplified by the unparalleled heroism they exhibited during the devastating terrorist attacks on 9/11, during which 23 NYPD officers died after rushing to the horrific scene to aid people. Dozens more have since succumbed to the incurable, mostly lung-related illnesses they contracted during the rescue operations at Ground Zero. These unflinching first responders helped save up to 25,000 others around the area that day.

On the opposite end of this rift are those who are anything but fond of the NYPD. Many critics consider the NYPD's reputation permanently marred by the scores of scandals that the department has been mired in since its very inception, including evidence tampering, various forms of corruption, and especially police brutality and violence stemming from institutional racism. Not only has the NYPD been accused of disproportionately targeting and harassing African-Americans, Muslims, and other minorities, one of its officers was involved in one of the many tragedies that propelled the rise of the Black Lives Matter movement. On July 17, 2014, a civilian named Eric Garner was cornered by the cops outside of a Staten Island beauty supply store. As seen in the viral video captured by one of Garner's friends, the officers attempted to apprehend the unarmed 43-year-old father of six for peddling untaxed cigarettes, otherwise known as "loosies." When Garner protested, maintaining his innocence, Officer Daniel Pantaleo tackled him from behind, and with the aid of four of his colleagues, Pantaleo locked the "suspect" in a chokehold for 15 seconds. Garner stated his now infamous utterance, "I can't breathe," not once, but 11 times, and yet his cries, muffled by the sidewalk, went unheard. Only when Garner lost consciousness did the officers finally roll him onto to his side and call for an ambulance. He died at the hospital about an hour later.

Despite the NYPD's policy against the use of chokeholds, the Staten Island jury selected for the case neglected to indict Pantaleo on criminal charges. Naturally, the public took to the streets to shine a light on this injustice, but that is another, albeit relevant story. Prosecutor Jonathan Fogel encapsulated the awfulness of this avoidable tragedy in three sentences: "A chokehold set off a domino effect that led to cardiac arrest that led to his death. It is an outrage that Eric Garner is not alive today. He was given a death sentence for loosies."

As this suggests, the NYPD's history is anything but straightforward. *The NYPD: The History and Legacy of the New York City Police Department* examines how the department took shape and grew, and some of the most important people and events in its history. Along with pictures depicting important people, places, and events, you will learn about the NYPD like never before.

New Amsterdam

During the 17th century, the Netherlands, despite having only 1.5 million people in 1600, became a global maritime and trading power. By contrast, France at that same time had 20 million people, Spain had 8 million, and England had 5 million. Nevertheless, Amsterdam became one of the most important urban centers in the world and the location of the world's first stock market, and Dutch merchant ships and pirates plied the Atlantic, the Indian Ocean and the Pacific. The Dutch acquired colonies in the East Indies, where they seized control of the spice trade from the Portuguese, and in the West Indies, they acquired a number of islands from the Spanish (several of which are still Dutch today). They became the only Westerners who were allowed to trade with Shogunate Japan from a small island next to Nagasaki. All of this imperialism generated enormous amounts of wealth that flowed into the Netherlands.

Starting out with the voyages of Columbus westward in 1492 and Vasco de Gama going east around the bottom of Africa in 1498, Spain and Portugal established territorial colonies in the Americas and trading posts in East Asia. To try to catch up with their enemies (Portugal was also ruled by the same King as Spain from 1580-1640) in the lucrative trading enterprises and to hurt them in other parts of the world, the Dutch first attempted to find a shorter route to the riches of the Orient by going north around Russia. Three expeditions backed by Amsterdam merchants that went looking for such a Northeast Passage in the 1590s, led by William Barents were failures, with Barents dying in the High Arctic in 1597.

Dutch success in ventures launched both east and west was aided greatly by the formation of two joint-stock companies: the East India Company (known by its Dutch initials, VOC) and the West India Company. The VOC was founded in 1602 and the WIC in 1621, and both companies were granted full trading monopolies by the Dutch government in the respective geographical zones assigned to them and acted there as *de facto* governing bodies, although under the supervision of the States General. The WIC's most profitable coup came when an admiral in their employ captured the entire Spanish silver fleet *en route* from Mexico to Seville in 1628. However, the principal source of the company's profits came from slavery, through the sugar plantations it operated in the Caribbean and South America and as the world's largest trans-Atlantic purveyor of slaves to the other colonial powers. As a result, both the VOC and the WIC would play roles in the history of New Amsterdam.

It is likely that the ships of other European nations --fishermen, traders and the like – made trips to the area that would give rise to New York City during the 16th century, but it was not until the 1609 voyage of the Englishman Henry Hudson, employed by Dutch merchants from the East India Company, that there were written records of the area, including records of encounters with the native inhabitants, the Lenni-Lenape. Hudson sailed in his *fluyt*, the *Half Moon*, with a crew of 18 or 20 men, partly Dutch and partly English, and they tried to find a Northeast Passage to the riches of China by going over the top of the world. His friend, Captain John Smith, one of the leaders of the new English colony at Jamestown, Virginia, had suggested that he might find something around latitude 40 degrees.

After surveying the coastline as far south as North Carolina and finding nothing, Hudson headed back north up the coast, where he arrived outside New York harbor on September 3. Hudson's and his men's interactions with the natives they encountered were mixed. When the *Half Moon* arrived near New York harbor, probably anchoring off Sandy Hook or Staten Island, Lenni-Lenape came out to their ship in canoes to trade with them, indicating in their behavior that this was something which they had done before. On the day after that, however, a boat sent out to explore and take soundings of the water depth had a violent scrape with some Lenni-Lenape warriors in two large boats, one carrying 12 men and the other with 14.

Meanwhile, the Lenni-Lenape had their own strong oral traditions of their encounter with Hudson and the *Half Moon* on Manhattan Island. These were collected by the Moravian missionary John Heckewelder, who spent a great deal of time with the Indians in the second half of the 18th century. According to Heckewelder's informants, the Indians who first spied Hudson's ship in the distance were stunned by what their eyes saw. Some concluded that the ship was an uncommonly large fish or some other animal, while others thought it was a very large house.

The news of Henry Hudson's discoveries, once they became known, aroused great interest in the Netherlands, but for whatever reason, the East India Company (VOC), which had sponsored his trip, did not follow up, probably because it was outside of its assigned geographical region. That task was taken up by other Amsterdam merchants, the bulk of whom were Lutheran refugees from the Catholic southern provinces that were still controlled by Spain. Several competing sets of merchants sent ships to the region starting in 1612, and they demonstrated the benefits of future ventures by returning with furs. This free-for-all was great for the Indians because the competition drove up the fur prices, but it was not so good for the different merchants who were unable to come to a fair agreement among themselves.

The first Dutch families arrived at New Amsterdam in 1624 and settled on *Noten Eylant* ("Nut Island"), which the Indians called "Pagganck" (the same meaning) because of its many chestnut, hickory, and oak trees. It's now known as Governor's Island. Some were sent out to Ft. Orange and outlying Dutch settlements on the Delaware River, but they were quickly pulled back for fear that they could not be defended or supported there.

A director appointed by the West India Company was the person on the scene in charge of trade and colonization, and he governed with the help of a council. Under the directorship of Willem Verhulst, construction began in 1625 on Ft. Amsterdam at the lower west bottom of Manhattan across from Governor's Island. Today, the seal of New York City, which depicts a Dutch sailor with his navigation tools, an Indian holding a bow, four windmills blades, two flour barrels and two beavers, marks that year, 1625, as the date of its founding.

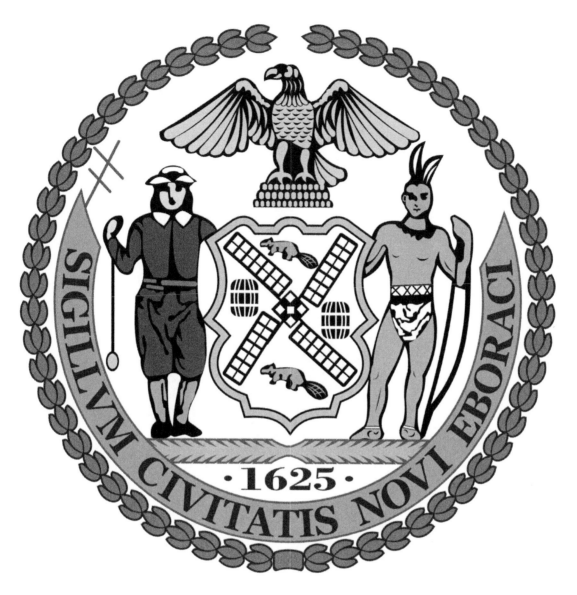

New York City's seal

Even so, it was not until the 1626 that Peter Minuit, the West India Company's next director, purchased Manhattan Island from the local Lenni-Lenape for 60 guilders worth of trade goods. This provides the origins of the fable about some of the most expensive real estate in the world being purchased for $24 (although that amount would be worth quite a bit more today). The Indians' concept of property was based on use-rights, not exclusivity, and that is probably what they thought they were agreeing to share. Staten Island (named for the *States General*) was acquired in a similar transaction in 1626, while the other great borough of what became New York City, Brooklyn, was acquired in 1646.

Minuit

A 1639 map shows more farms and plantations existing by that time on Manhattan north to Morningside Heights and Harlem, across the Hudson in what is now New Jersey, and on Long Island. Tobacco was grown on some of the plantations, and ever since the 17th century, the area of lower Manhattan east of today's Little Italy and north of Chinatown has been known as "the Bowery," deriving its name from the old Dutch word for farms ("bouwerji"). The 1639 map also shows a grist mill and a saw mill existing close by the fort and another saw mill located out on Governor's Island. Ft. Amsterdam was completed in 1635. It consisted of a brick interior with an earth and turf exterior. The shape of the fort, following state-of-the-art European military design, was a quadrangle with a bastion at each of the four corners. Along with protecting the colony from attack, another important task of the authorities was to establish a church. The first communion in a Dutch Reformed Church under Rev. Jonas Michaelius took place in 1628; the first church building was built in 1633.

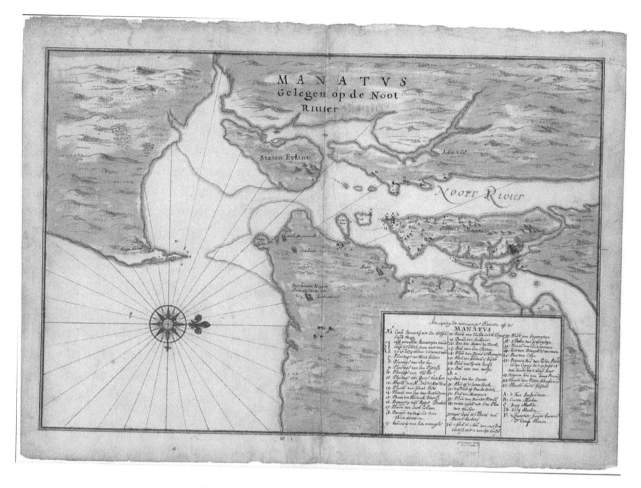

The 1639 map of New Amsterdam

To attract more settlers to New Netherland, the West India Company instituted a new policy in 1629 whereby wealthy individuals and groups of individuals could be granted large pieces of the colony's territory and essentially become feudal lords – *patroons* – with almost total authority over that territory and its inhabitants. In order to become a *patroon,* what one needed to do was to agree to bring 50 adults to an area of the colony that was not Manhattan within a period of four years. Their fiefdom could extend 16 miles along a navigable river or eight miles on both sides and an unlimited distance into the backcountry. Settlers would be rent-paying tenants who could not leave without the permission of the *patron*, and *patroons* held a monopoly on hunting, fishing and milling grain.

The Dutch tried to maintain good relations with all of the tribes for the sake of healthy trade but found themselves in the middle of conflicts among some of them, conflicts exacerbated by the fur trade. At Ft. Orange on the upper Hudson River, the powerful Mohawks of the Iroquois Confederacy challenged the Mahicans for access to the Dutch traders and attempted to become the middlemen with more inland tribes, so the Mahicans were forced to cede their land and relocate to the eastern side of the river.

As Dutch populations grew and expanded, the Indians became increasingly upset. By 1640, the Dutch had spread out from Manhattan and established new settlements on Staten Island, Long Island, and in the Bronx, which was named for Jonas Bronck after he settled there in 1639. They also settled in what is now Westchester County and New Jersey.

Given all that, the colony's founders rightly anticipated the need for some form of policing from almost the very beginning. Minuit's predecessor, Willem Verhulst, created the post of *schout-fiscal*, or "sheriff-attorney," in 1625, and appointed a man identified only as "Johann" for the job. The *schout-fiscal*, as the title suggests, served as both police and prosecutor. In addition to monitoring the main streets and enforcing the company's laws, he was tasked with maintaining civil order, mediating minor disputes, and counseling colonists during fires and other emergencies.

It did not take long for the authorities to accept and rectify the deficiencies of the simplistic system. Not surprisingly, one lone official, assisted by random volunteers, was ill-equipped to cater to the needs of the growing settlements. Burgher guards, essentially private bodyguards for the privileged class, rose to popularity in the two decades that followed, but these hired minders only had the interests of their employers in mind, so they did little to improve the overall security of the colony.

When Willem Kieft arrived as New Amsterdam's director in 1638, it was already a sort of den of iniquity, full of "mischief and perversity," where residents were given over to smoking and drinking grog and beer. Under Kieft's reign, more land was acquired mostly through bloody, all-but-exterminating wars with the Native American population, whose numbers also dwindled at the hands of European diseases.

In March 1644, the Wecquaesgeeks and Wappingers made peace with the Dutch. In August 1645 a general peace treaty was signed at New Amsterdam by Kieft and his council, with some Lenni-Lenape sachems agreeing that further conflicts would be settled not through violence but through complaints taken to the sachems and the Dutch authorities. To reduce chances for violence, the treaty specified that Indians would not come into New Amsterdam, nor would the Dutch come into the Indian villages with their guns.

The Rattle Watch

"Musket on shoulder and dirk on thigh,

Forth from the fort with a soulful sigh...

Smite with your rattles the startled ear!

Let every miscreant know you're near...

Come, merry lover of sights and sounds,

Follow the Watch on their nightly rounds!" – Arthur Guiterman, "The Rattle Watch of New Amsterdam"

The peace treaty with the Lenni-Lenape held, but ultimately, Kieft was removed from his position as colony director, and on his way back home to Amsterdam to try to justify his conduct, his ship was lost at sea. The new director replacing Kieft was Peter Stuyvesant, with whom New Netherland would be associated for the rest of its existence until it was taken over by the English in 1664. Under his tenure, there would be two further wars between other Indian tribes and the Dutch: the "Peach War" with the Susquehannocks in 1655 and a long war with the Esopus from 1659-1663.

Stuyvesant

Things were not much more civilized in New Amsterdam when Stuyvesant took over in 1647. The residents, to him, had "grown wild and were loose in their morals." With his peg leg in tow (part of Stuyvesant's right leg had been amputated due to a cannonball hit during his stint in the

Caribbean), the staunch Calvinist began to make some serious changes. No longer could livestock roam free with abandon, or garbage be thrown into the streets, which were now to be paved in cobblestones (the first such street was the now aptly named Stone Street). Dangerous wooden chimneys and other combustible building materials were outlawed, and a sort of fire department was established. However, alms for the poor, orphanages, and schools received less or grudging support—as they continue to do today. Many decrees were issued; in fact, the first law against driving too fast was passed in 1657. Stuyvesant's "civilizing" mission helped a new, more regulated and stratified society form, one with a newly wealthy merchant class and, of course, many classes below them.

The peg-legged Director-General Stuyvesant also sought to ameliorate the colony's worsening public safety issue by establishing the first municipal police force on August 12, 1658. The *ratel wacht*, or "rattle watch," is now considered a progenitor of the NYPD. The force was aptly named after the distinctive hardwood rattles the watchmen toted, which were somewhat pistol-shaped contraptions that consisted of ribbed, bowling pin-like handles, a cogwheel, and a clapper. The following names were listed on the roster of the nine-man troop: Hendrick van Bommel, Pieter Jansen, Jan Jansen van Lang-straat, Jan Pietersen, Gerrit Pietersen, Jacques Pryn, Hendrick Ruyter, Tomas Verdran, and Jan Cornelsen van Vlensburg.

Stuyvesant's systematic approach to public security seemed to bear fruit. Whereas the *schout-fiscal* and his assistants were only available at odd hours, the rattle watch patrolled at a fixed schedule, typically from dusk to dawn, making for more effective policing. The watchmen were not issued specific uniforms, but they were required to carry distinguishable accessories, so they could be identified by civilians. Rattles aside, the watchmen stalked the streets with the poles of their green lanterns slung over their shoulders, and they were armed with flintlock muskets and pistols, cudgels, and other weapons. Civilians, for the most part, began to associate the rattles and the green glows of the lanterns, which could be spotted floating around in the pre-streetlight dark of the night like fireflies, with authority. The watchmen clocked in by hanging a separate set of lanterns outside the doors of the watch house. The tradition lives on today, as two emerald-green lamps are mounted on either side of the entrances of all major NYPD police stations, symbolizing the watch's constant vigilance.

The primary duty of the rattle watch, as per Stuyvesant's orders, was to watch over the colony, and to be on the lookout for "pirates, vagabonds, and robbers." The watchmen were also expected to break up physical and verbal altercations, prevent loitering, and spook the intoxicated off the streets. Moreover, one or two of the watchmen were posted by the city gates to peel off the villagers who attempted to scale the city wall, which ran along what is now Wall Street. Civilians caught doing so were marched to the whipping post, and repeat offenders were sentenced to the gallows, though to what extent the death penalty was enforced in such cases is unclear.

Interestingly enough, the watchmen's weapons, loaded with "six charges of ammunition," were little more than props. The *ratel wacht* was not trained to deal with confrontation, but to essentially act as walking alarm systems and deterrents, not proactive fighters of crime. The watchmen's instincts were not to reach for their arms, but their rattles, which they cranked repeatedly, producing a string of jarring and unnerving clicking sounds. The racket was usually all it took to scare off potential criminals and stop passersby in their tracks.

The rattle watch expanded accordingly with the colony's rising population. Burghers were conscripted and summoned to duty on rotation, and those caught sidestepping their summons were reprimanded and fined. Those who were discovered sleeping on the job or sporting a rumpled shirt and poor hygiene were also fined, with the former offense setting watchmen back 10 stuyvers (roughly $7.50 today).

Penalizing misbehaving watchmen via fines appeared to be a significant part of the *ratel wacht* culture. The following are a few of the rules that the watchmen were expected to abide by, as documented by James Dabney McCabe in *New York by Sunlight and Gaslight* (1881): "When anyone comes on the watch being drunk, or is in any way insolent or unreasonable in his behavior, he shall be committed to the square-room or to the battlements of the town hall, and shall besides pay six stuyvers...If anyone be heard to blaspheme the name of God, he shall forfeit 10 stuyvers...If anyone attempts to fight when on the watch, or tries to draw off from the watch for the purpose of fighting, he shall forfeit two guilders ($30)." The fines may seem inconsequential, but they were liberally imposed, which added up quite quickly.

On average, the watchmen were compensated a modest 24 stuyvers ($17.40) for an evening's work. Alternatively, some watchmen opted instead for "one or two beavers...and two or three hundred sticks of firewood" in exchange for their services. The watchmen's salaries were funded by the colonists themselves. Ludowyck Pos, who was later elected captain of the rattle watch, collected 50 stuyvers from every residence on the first week of each month.

The *ratel wacht* was indeed a promising concept on paper, but it was rife with imperfections and poorly executed, which ultimately led to its demise. Funding shortages, the faulty recruitment system, and ineffectual leadership resulted in abrupt hiatuses and inconsistent performance on the watchmen's part, meaning that crime rates and public morale suffered.

Ultimately, the constant litany of complaints filed against the watchmen – submitted by their superiors, colleagues, and the public –sealed the rattle watch's fate. Not unlike the countless accusations of misconduct that the NYPD has always faced, the rattle watchmen, especially the later generations, flouted the watch's stance against conflict and were criticized for their use of excessive force. Others failed to resist the allure of bribery and corruption.

The watch's recruitment methods raised many an eyebrow from the first day. Prior to the burgher conscription system, petty criminals and other civilians with misdemeanors on their records were employed as punishment for their transgressions, making them a community service of sorts. Burghers replaced the small-time crooks, holding the rattles for the better part of the late 17th century, but come the 1700s, mandatory enlistment was extended to all social classes, normally the breadwinners of every colonial family.

Curiously, women were not exempt from the rattle watch rotation. A 1734 court document details the case of a woman who was repeatedly issued a series of summons, and as such, she sought restitution for the sizable sums she was made to fork over for the substitutes she hired in her place. The plaintiff, Deborah Careful, lamented to the press, "[I] have been forced to pay as much as the richest man in town, though God knows I can hardly buy my bread; however, I was told, I must do it, till there was an Act of Assembly to remedy the Devil."

Careful's concerns were pitiable, but the fact that she, or anyone summoned, was even permitted to hire a substitute was itself a problem. These proxies were often questionable, unreliable characters who were more interested in the cash than they were the job. That being said, the summoned who reported for duty were, more often than not, equally substandard, presumably due to the absence of a proper vetting process.

The watchmen themselves were accused of rowdiness and unabashed day-drinking. It was apparently not uncommon to witness a watchman relieving himself or passed out on the steps of *Stadt Huys* ("City Hall"). Needless to say, both the judgment and performance of the inebriated patrolmen were compromised - they frequently neglected (or declined) to sound their rattles when needed, allowing criminals to slip past them and delaying critical announcements.

Others played malicious pranks on the townspeople. Some of the watchmen, who doubled as town criers for some time, for instance, woke civilians before dawn. When the victims of the practical jokers lodged complaints, they retaliated by withholding the wake-up calls altogether.

The watchmen were also slated for their reported refusal to patrol certain streets. The residents of Pearl Street, for one, called the watchmen out for their negligence and subsequently stopped paying the taxes that funded their salaries. A 1757 article from the *New York Gazette* contains a revealing quote from an anonymous civilian: "[The watchmen] are a parcel of idle, drinking, vigilant snorers, who never quelled any nocturnal tumult in their lives; nor, as we can learn, were ever the discoverers of a fire breaking out, but would perhaps be as ready to join in a burglary as any thief in Christendom."

Whenever the weight of the public backlash became too much to bear, authorities caved in and temporarily swapped out the watchmen for military men. Unfortunately, the colonial government was unable to shoulder the costs of these well-trained, highly qualified professionals, so this was no more than a stopgap measure. The reorganization the colony's law enforcement desperately needed only came to pass after the American Revolution.

The Early Years of the NYPD

Shortly after the signing of the Treaty of Paris in early September 1783, which effectively ended the Revolutionary War and formally recognized America's independence, the government of New York scrapped the *ratel wacht* and rolled out an extensive new night watch system. 300 porters, longshoremen, and other middle-class laborers were hired en masse, and in contrast to their antecedents, the new evening guardsmen applied for these positions and were provided with similar (albeit still primitive) training. Gone were the rattles and green lanterns; now, the new watchmen were issued 33-inch clubs, as well as leather fireman's hats with irregularly shaped, upturned brims and onion-like crowns, minus the large brass plates. They were required to shellac their hats no less than twice a year, which hardened their headgear over time. As such, they were colloquially referred to as "Leather-heads," as well as "Old Charlies."

While there was a noticeable improvement in the Old Charlies' diligence, they were far too spent from their day jobs, which took a toll on their nightly duties. What's more, the sluggish watchmen struck little to no fear in local criminals, for they were regarded as pushovers who could be easily overpowered. A healthy fraction of the watchmen equipped with greater stamina, though credible citizens of good repute, were more invested in the potential prize money in store for them, such as collecting rewards for the stolen possessions they located and retrieved.

More importantly, authorities experimented with a more assertive subsidiary patrol for the first time. Armed constables, usually accompanied by two or three other deputies, were instructed to monitor the streets both day and night, actively solving crimes and resolving disputes on their daily beats. Marshals were also separately employed to serve and enforce warrants. One constable per district initially sufficed; in later years, two constables, along with a high constable, were assigned to each ward.

Predictably, the enhanced patrol force mitigated crime rates, but they continued to be held in low regard, as the unsavory reputation they had garnered in their rattle watch days was more abiding than they had anticipated. This was the situation when Constable Jacob Hays took command and transformed their posts into positions of power and authority. In short, if the rattle watch and constables were progenitors, Hays is considered by many the father of the NYPD.

Hays, a Sephardic Jew, started his career in law enforcement as an unpaid marshal in 1797, supposedly at the recommendation of none other than Attorney General Aaron Burr. Notwithstanding his lack of a salary and the simplicity of his job description, which mainly involved secretarial bureaucratic tasks, he assiduously attended to his duties and was eventually promoted to the commission-based position of constable of the 5th Ward. In addition to peacekeeping and occasionally rounding up farm animals that had escaped their pens, Hays enforced Sabbath laws, which prohibited the sale and consumption of alcohol, firecracker play, and other recreational activities on Sundays.

Burr

Rather than protest or strike against the discouraging commission-dependent income those in law enforcement received, the perceptive Hays chose to prove their worth. To begin with, Hays established a kind of criminal database consisting of individual files on offenders, complete with a list of their past delinquencies and a crude description of said criminals. The 5th Ward's middling population likely made it easier for its constables and watchmen to preserve order. Hays, in particular, made it a point to familiarize himself with the local criminals, and they certainly got to know him.

Hays' efforts did not go unnoticed. He was appointed High Constable by Mayor Edward Livingston in 1802, but to his disappointment, the stipend he was granted did not bear the luster of his title, equivalent only to the salary of a low-ranking clerk. He tolerated the paltry pay for about a year or two, but as a firm believer of the connection between pay and productivity, he soon petitioned for proper constabulary wages and was finally awarded a raise in 1812.

Livingston

The high constable spared no effort in reconstructing the tarnished image of the New York patrolmen, and it showed. He befriended and maintained solid relationships with local journalists, who published multiple articles regarding Hays and his heroics, which helped to cast the constables in a whole new light. The high constable was portrayed as a gruff and no-nonsense, yet honest and fearless roundsman whose mere name was enough to make children and criminals alike quiver in their boots. Career criminals were well-aware of Hays' highly publicized gift: his extraordinary facial recognition skills. As one journalist put it, "Half a look [was] enough for old Jacob." Parents also capitalized on Hays' fierce features, specifically his bushy eyebrows and pronounced aquiline nose, permanently accompanied by a crumpled forehead and scowl, and turned him into a bogeyman. They would warn their children, "Behave or watch out, because Old Hays will get you!"

Eventually, it was Hays' dedication to pursuing leads and cracking cases, possessing many of the qualities associated with the then-emerging field of detective work, that made him a household name. Hays took the initiative to take on cases and assumed responsibilities beyond his pay grade. He specialized in busting counterfeiting rings, at times tracking fraud syndicates outside of New York, and even the country. In 1818, Hays unraveled a massive counterfeiting operation based in rural Ontario, foiling their plans to smuggle $100,000 (approximately $2.98 million today) in false bills into the United States.

The following excerpt, taken from an 1834 article, recounts another one of Hays' triumphant exploits: "Before noon on Wednesday...Hays, with the sole assistance of his son Benjamin, and with no other clue to the thieves than his own shrewdness and natural sagacity furnished, had recovered the greater part of the property, which was buried in the earth about six miles from the city...the ensuing day, Benjamin Hays arrested two of the thieves, in whose possession he found the remainder of the property, except two watches."

At this stage, New York City's population of roughly 320,000 lay under the protection of 400 night watchmen, 100 city marshals, 31 constables, and 51 deputies. Hays may have steered the ship around, but the vessel continued to pummeled by high crime rates. Celebrated poet Walt Whitman referred to New York as "one of the most crime-haunted and dangerous cities in Christendom." The influx of displaced criminals that had wandered in from neighboring and faraway cities, Whitman explained, contributed to the escalating hooliganism in New York. According to Whitman, "These were thieves expelled, some of them, from distant San Francisco (post-Gold Rush) vomited back among us to practice their criminal occupations." The Long Island native's trust in the local patrol force remained minute, and he urged visitors to employ extra caution when traveling around the city, warning, "Any affable stranger who makes friendly offers is very likely to attempt to swindle you as soon as he can get into your confidence. Mind your own business."

Much like Whitman, law enforcement officers pinned the blame on the city's rapidly swelling census. By 1855, the year of Whitman's remarks, the population had skyrocketed to 629,810, and would it would reach close to a million in less than a decade. To put this in perspective, the city was home to only 60,000, mostly condensed in southern Manhattan, just 55 years prior.

The overworked patrolmen began a collective campaign for a larger, more structured force. Unable to ignore these vigorous appeals, Mayor William Havemeyer and his cabinet, the Board of Aldermen, relayed the matter to Governor William C. Bouck, who finally acquiesced.

Havemeyer

Alas, this new and improved police force that would soon come to fruition failed to maintain the template that Hays had so painstakingly constructed. Patrick Bringley, author of *The Irresistible Invitation of High Constable Jacob Hays: A Career Policing New York*, explained that "in important ways, [Hays] innovated, but mainly he was a 'last lion,' a figure whose fame derived in part from his unlikely success, and also perhaps from an elegiac awareness that his like would not be seen again. Hays policed New York at a time when it was becoming unpoliceable [sic]... The police department that succeeded Hays was not a collection of superheroes – it was impersonal, bureaucratized, uniform, and uniformed, the very antithesis of Old Hays..."

Taking into account Bringley's strong sentiments, the official birthday of the modern-day NYPD, which took place closely after the retirement of the feared, yet beloved High Constable Hays, could not have been more fitting.

On May 7, 1844, the state legislature approved a proposal that authorized the formation of the New York City Police Department and the abolition of the antiquated night watch wing. Officials were resolved to assemble a full-scale, superlative crime fighting force with all the bells and whistles, one that could deal with the kingpins of the New York underworld. To do so,

Havemayer and the Common Council sought consultation from the renowned Peter Cooper, the inventor, industrialist, and philanthropist behind the *Tom Thumb*, America's first steam locomotive. Cooper, who authored the proposal, suggested a starting crew comprised of a minimum of 1,200 officers.

Cooper

On May 13, 1845, Mayor Havemayer instituted a few changes, the most significant of them being the division of the city into three districts, each to be ruled by its own unit of NYPD officers, magistrates, and clerks. The new police department, supposedly the first of its kind in the United States, held their grand opening two months later. Havemayer only managed to muster together 800 men, 400 short from Cooper's ideal 1,200, but all the same, the 800 officers were inducted that morning. They vowed to defer to the leadership of George Washington Matsell, the first Police Commissioner of the NYPD.

Matsell

The 37-year-old Matsell was the son of an ambitious immigrant from Norfolk, England who settled in New York City in the final years of the 18th century and erected a small tailor shop on the corner of Broadway Street. In his 20s, the restless Matsell took shallow stabs at various professions, including an apprenticeship at his father's tailor shop, and he even embarked on numerous voyages for a few years during his sailor phase. Once the siren song of the sea lost its magnetism, Matsell returned to the city and opened up a bookshop of his own, so it wasn't until his late 20s or early 30s that he stumbled upon his calling.

Matsell, a registered Democrat, tested the waters of politics for some time, and in 1840 he found employment as a police magistrate. Still, the jack of all trades remained unfulfilled, so he chose to uplift himself with a side project. The observant magistrate took it upon himself to appraise the fruitfulness of the city's constables and watchmen, and when he found himself appalled by the incompetence of the patrolmen and the disorganization of the old-fangled system, he started his own unofficial detective agency. Matsell's sleuths operated mostly along the riverfront, uncovering clues and unmasking suspects, leading to dozens of arrests. The amateur detectives were apparently so proficient and Matsell's captaincy was so potent that they served as muses for the reforms in Havemeyer and Cooper's proposal. Clearly, the city council concluded, Matsell was perfect for the job.

The NYPD was consciously patterned after the London Metropolitan Police Service, its designers intrigued by militarized nature of the English crime force. Thus, the NYPD adopted many of the same rank titles, including Police Commissioner/Chief, Chief Inspector, Inspector, Captain, Detective Sergeant, Sergeant, Roundsman, and finally, Patrolman. The officers were also issued their first badges, as described by the *Station Bay* blog in this passage: "[The Patrolman badge] was in the shape of an eight-pointed star (representing the eight original members of the Dutch *ratel wacht*) with a circle in the center that holds a design consisting of a coat of arms with a windmill on it. On either side of the coat of arms is a man, one being a Native American. Perched above the coat of arms is an eagle, and below the word 'police.' The Patrolman police badge was made out of brass. The department issued the same design in a white metal for Sergeants...same design was also placed inside a ring to indicate Assistant Captain."

The NYPD badge experienced several alterations throughout the years, but it maintained a similar overall aesthetic, with one exception being the short-lived "Potsy" badge that was introduced in the latter years of the 19th century. The centerpiece was no longer the coat of arms, which was shrunken down and placed in the upper left corner of the rectangular tin shield, but instead the words "POLICE DEPARTMENT," followed by the precinct number and title of the officer in bold, embossed lettering.

Of course, no institution would be complete without its own motto. The department settled on the Latin phrase *Fidelis ad Mortem,* which translates into "Faithful unto Death."

John Watts de Peyster, the Adjutant General of New York and a decorated veteran who served in the New York State Militia during the Mexican-American War and the Civil War, played an instrumental role in designing standardized training courses for the unversed officers. They would be whipped into shape via military-grade discipline, a part of which entailed the re-education of these recruits, many of them former city guards. During such re-educational sessions, the fresh recruits were taught to banish the outdated techniques of the constables and watchmen, and the ex-patrolmen to forget everything that they had learned. The constables, their superiors reasoned, had not been rendered obsolete without valid reason. They were physically and mentally weak, spoiled by the overly lax management, and allowed themselves to be intimidated by the very scum they had sworn to sweep off the streets. The recruits were urged to toughen up and fight back and were authorized to implement as much force as they saw fit, should the situation call for it. Behind the scenes, some claimed, the trainees were encouraged to threaten potentially belligerent criminals with their weapons, so as to assert their dominance.

De Peyster

    The new mentality the trainers attempted to instill in the recruits was certainly controversial, akin to fighting fire with fire, but its advocates, burdened by increasing public pressure and the ever-expanding prowess of New York's criminals, felt that the city had exhausted all its other options. To be fair, the concept of "necessary force" itself was not the problem; the issue was that the trainers lacked the foresight to set limits and regulations in stone, in essence allowing the new officers to run amok, clubs and pistols in hand, bound by no repercussions. Many made a habit of clobbering criminals over the head or striking them on the nape of their necks with their chunky, 14-inch-long billy clubs at the slightest provocation. Suspects, persons of interest, and demonstrators alike were seized by their collars, dragged across the coarse pavement, and shoved into police wagons. An early 20th century patrolman named Cornelius Willemse once mused, "They were powerful, fearless men who dispensed the law with a nightstick, seldom bothering to make arrests."

The interrogated were slammed against walls, kicked down flights of stairs, and subjected to chokeholds, ear-pulling, finger-twisting, and knees to the groin and other sensitive areas. Those manhandled by the officers were often knocked unconscious, and in the worst cases they were permanently crippled or suffered brain damage.

When the officers tired of these more mainstream forms of violence, they resorted to creatively cruel forms of punishment. An unnamed woman who was apprehended at a boardinghouse in Manhattan, for instance, was made to strip off her shoes and speed-march for over a mile to the Tyron Row jail in the midst of a severe thunderstorm. All the while, the NYPD's wildly problematic interrogation techniques, referred to as the "third degree," was brushed off as yet another necessary evil.

The contentious issue divided public opinion. Supporters of the policy applauded authorities for, at long last, setting in motion a plan to crush crime, and they deemed the use of force a regrettable, but integral part of the compromise. Naysayers, on the other hand, denounced the practice, predicting the problematic path that lay ahead. According to Robert J. Livingston of the esteemed Livingston Family, "Officers of justice, often uneducated or overbearing men, either do not know or designedly [sic] exceed the boundaries of their authority. The accused sometimes submits to illegal acts; in others, resists those to whom he ought to submit." Protesters also cited the recent killing of an innocent bystander in Philadelphia, who was shot when he attempted to intervene on behalf of a suspect who was in the process of being arrested.

Some viewed the naysayers' opinions as constructive criticism and dialed back the aggression they employed when confronting criminals. Others rationalized the need for saber-rattling tactics, but once they felt the heat of the public outcry, took extra steps to conceal their unpopular methods. These combative officers, for starters, bandaged their clubs with two handkerchief squares to prevent the formation of bruises and suspicious marks. Moving forward, suspects were viciously beaten behind the closed doors of jailhouses or in empty, dimly lit alleys, where there were no witnesses, only participants.

Even more concerning, the police urged civilians not only to defend themselves from their assailants, but to initiate attacks against their tormentors. Captain George Walling advised a civilian involved in a property line dispute to assault his neighbor, and when the civilian in question balked at Walling's solution, the captain egged him on and guaranteed his freedom. The following day, the civilian lunged at his neighbor and slugged him repeatedly, beating the man beyond recognition. The neighbor conceded defeat and kept his distance from there on out. Walling denied any involvement in the gratuitous attack, but similar accusations continued to be leveled against him throughout the remainder of his career.

As controversial as the tactics were, criminals reportedly began to think twice about tackling police officers and resisting arrest, with a few even shrinking away from illegal activities altogether. The public's conception of the city's crime force had unquestionably been altered - the cops were no longer regarded as easy game or listless drunks, but ferocious, menacing browbeaters on a quest to eradicate the scourge of New York City. They may not have yet gained the respect of their charges, but they certainly secured the command and power that they had so craved.

Despite, or perhaps because of the police's renewed zeal to reacquire control over the city's streets, they were not infallible. On July 22, 1849, Patrolman Thomas Lynch was dispatched to 16 Dover Street to investigate a report regarding a violent dispute. Lynch wedged himself between the brawling men in an attempt to deescalate the situation, but the aggressor turned on the patrolman, who sustained 11 incapacitating iron pipe blows to the head. He succumbed to his injuries on September 27th, making him the first NYPD officer killed in the line of duty.

Authorities discovered that it took less effort to blame scapegoats than it did to contend with the city's crime problem. The city, authorities claimed, had become overrun by hordes of Irish immigrants, the majority of them guileful crooks and barbaric thugs who not only exacerbated, but were in large part the catalysts of the staggering crime wave. Thus, the Irish were disproportionately vulnerable to the NYPD's policy of "necessary force."

A little over a million displaced Irish immigrants poured into the city between 1845 and 1852, and by the end of the century, one out of every four New Yorkers was Irish. The Irish had boldly risked their lives to escape the devastating poverty and starvation engendered by the wretched Great Famine, which wiped out over a million civilians and prompted the mass emigration of a million more. Whatever solace they sought, sadly, could not be found in New York, as they were deemed reprehensible pests that brought nothing but trouble and suffering. Other neighbors simply took offense to the Irish's Catholic faith.

A derogatory political cartoon published in the April 6, 1867 issue of *Harper's Weekly,* entitled "The Day We Celebrate," succinctly captures the prejudices of 19th century New Yorkers. In this Thomas Nast original, the Irish were depicted as apelike, sharp-toothed humanoids attacking NYPD officers at a Saint Patrick's Day celebration, stomping on the heads of the patrolmen, bashing their faces in with clubs, and yanking fistfuls of their hair.

ST. PATRICKS DAY 1867.

RUM. BRUTAL ATTACK ON THE POLICE "THE DAY WE CELEBRATE." IRISH RIOT. Th. Nast. BLOOD.

The cartoon

The authorities, likewise, made no efforts to hide how much they despised the Irish. The Irish immigrants were crammed into their own districts and forced to live in inhumane conditions, to the point that throughout the 1860s, close to 300,000 Irish civilians occupied one measly square mile, stuffed into shoddily made structures carelessly stacked on top of one another. Five large families, averaging about 20 people in total, were made to shack up in a single sparsely furnished room no larger than an above-average sized bedroom for one. An 1865 report noted, "In [these] tenant-house districts, a worse than Spartan fate awaits all children, and cholera infantum, convulsions, scrofula, and marasmus hover with ghoul-like fiendishness..."

What lay outside these unimaginably cramped apartments was far worse. An 1863 article from the *New York Tribune* painted a disturbing picture of the scene outside, which consisted of "...potato-peelings...night-soil, rancid butter, dead dogs and cats strewn across the streets....one festering, rotting, loathsome, hellish mass of air poisoning, death-breeding filth." Adding insult to injury, the Irish were charged exorbitant rent fees, which surpassed the rates of houses in decent neighborhoods.

As might be expected, many Irishmen, who faced rejection from xenophobic landlords and employers ad nauseam, chased their sorrows away with booze. Many began to associate alcohol abuse, violence, and other forms of destructive behavior with the immigrant population, and conspiracy theories surrounding the Irish only fueled the mass hysteria. The Irish, these rumor mills claimed, were kidnapping women and holding them hostage in Catholic convents, where they were forced into nunhood. There, they were beaten and raped by the priests, and the children they bore were then strangled upon birth, thereby eliminating the evidence of their unholy relations.

The NYPD used these rumors as ammunition to further their anti-Irish and anti-Catholic campaigns. The Irish shared the tales of harassment they endured at the hands of the police officers, and many were wrongfully arrested for gang affiliation, but their protests landed on deaf ears. New Yorkers were either willfully ignorant or apathetic towards the plight of their Irish compatriots.

Meanwhile, the NYPD wrestled with the rampancy of another unlikely, but all the same concerning group of criminals: vagrant and delinquent children. Describing them as "embryo courtesans and felons," Matsell's 1849 annual report told its readers, "I deem it my duty, to call the attention of Your Honor to a deplorable and growing evil which exists amid this community....for which the laws and ordinances afford no adequate remedy. I allude to the constantly increasing number of vagrants, idle and vicious children of both sexes, who infest our public thoroughfares, hotels, docks, etc...Reports have been made to me from the captains of the First, Second, Third, Fourth, Fifth, Sixth, Seventh, Eighth, Tenth, Eleventh, and Thirteenth Patrol districts, from which it appears that the enormous number of 2,955 children are engaged as above described in these wards alone...Besides these, there are reported to me from the above named districts, 2,383 children that do not attend school."

In a twist few saw coming, it was not the Irish, nor the vagrant and delinquent youths, but the problematic institution itself that spelled the department's ruin. In the spring of 1857, Republicans in the state capital of Albany succeeded in passing a law that authorized disbanding of Havemeyer's Municipal police force and establishing the Metropolitan police force, citing the irremediable corruption within Mayor Fernando Wood's Tammany Hall and the NYPD. The newfound Metropolitan force unified the police departments of New York City, Staten Island, Brooklyn, and Westchester County into one unit, which was to be governed by a five-man board of commissioners consisting of James Bowen, Jacob Cholwell, Simeon Draper, James W. Nye, and James S. T. Stranahan.

Wood

The Metropolitan bill called for Mayor Wood to relinquish all property and resources of the Municipal force at once, but much to the Republicans' dismay, Wood refused to acknowledge the ordinance and demobilize the Municipal body. Thus, in the months that followed, New York was regulated by two separate police entities between the state-operated Metropolitans and Wood's Municipals. The state failed to foresee the Municipals' fidelity to the mayor, as 15 police captains and over 800 officers from the original Municipal force of 1,100 rallied behind Wood, whereas only 300 officers, along with 7 captains, including Captain Walling, went over to the Metropolitan force. The Metropolitans were easily outnumbered, and the rest of the new force was made up of unqualified, inexperienced first-timers.

In theory, with two active police departments, the streets of New York should have been the safest they had been in decades, but rather than set their differences aside and join forces for the greater good, the two parties proceeded to engage in turf wars that only added to the disarray. The poisonous infighting was not lost on the city's criminals, who immediately took advantage of the distractions. Robberies, lootings, murders, and gang-related violence skyrocketed, and in many cases, suspects arrested by one force would be liberated just hours later by the other. In one case, a suspect who was apprehended for public intoxication and disorderly conduct spurned the authority of his Metropolitan arresting officers and only complied when an unlicensed Municipal officer arrived at the scene. The Metropolitans accused the Municipals of accepting bribes from civilians in exchange for lenient sentences and other preferential treatment (hence their compliance), and they accused the Municipals of conspiring against the state-appointed force.

The confusion was further heightened by the perplexingly similar uniforms of the rival police forces. Both sets were navy-blue paramilitary ensembles reminiscent of the uniforms worn by the London "Bobbies," which included tailored double-breasted, waist-length coats and badges prominently displayed on the left of their chests. The chin straps of the flat-topped caps worn by the Municipal patrolmen and the floppy-brimmed fireman's helmets donned by high-ranking Municipal officers, as well as the white stripe that ran along the side of the Metropolitan officers' slacks were the only distinguishable features of the otherwise identical outfits.

CAPTAIN.　　CAP-COVER FOR RAIN.　　CHIEF.　　RESERVE CORPS.　　LIEUTENANT.　　PRIVATE.

NEW REGULATION UNIFORM OF THE NEW YORK POLICE.

The uniforms for the Municipals in 1857

On July 2, 1857, the Court of Appeals reiterated the Supreme Court's decision and ordered Wood to dissolve the Municipal force. To appease the courts, Wood publicly relented and made a show of surrendering major police stations to the Metropolitans, but in reality, the Municipals remained very much intact, with the center of their operations merely relocated to City Hall. Public reaction was swift, as Municipal supporters blasted the authorities for needlessly scrapping a perfectly effective system run by seasoned veterans and replacing it with an untested body of inexperienced novices, many using the mayhem that unfolded just two days later to push their points across.

The Independence Day festivities were interrupted by the outbreak of a bloody turf war. On the evening of July 4, the Irish Dead Rabbits gang, accompanied by assorted thugs from different Five Points gangs, arrived at The Bowery's Bayard Street. The nativist Bowery Boys and the Atlantic Guards, who controlled this portion of Southern Manhattan, defended their territory, and thanks to the absence of immediate police intervention, the scuffle spiraled into pandemonium across the city. Ruffians and civilians alike partook in the free-for-all, which spilled into the next day, engaging in more street rumbles, lootings, and arson sprees.

A unit of Metropolitan officers eventually arrived to quell the tumult, but the unseasoned Metropolitans, as noble as their intentions were, proved unable to handle a riot of this size. They were quickly subdued by Dead Rabbit gangsters, and, to make the embarrassing episode even more humiliating, they had to be saved by the Bowery Boys.

This incident, now referred to as the "Dead Rabbits Riot" or the "Independence Day Riot of 1857," was closely followed by yet another humbling experience that only served to worsen the negative publicity surrounding the Metropolitans. On July 12, German New Yorkers in the Lower East Side's *Kleindeutschland,* otherwise known as "Little Germany," started a rampage against the state-appointed officers in response to their enforcement of unwelcome liquor laws and shutdowns of local watering holes. The following day, 10,000 German New Yorkers and allies swarmed Broadway Street to protest the death of a blacksmith, who was killed in the crossfire. As they chanted for justice and paraded around Midtown Manhattan, they raised their large banners for all to see. Written across these canvases were the words *Opfer der Metropolitan-Polizei* ("Victim of the Metropolitan Police").

The rivalry between the rival police forces reached another crescendo less than two weeks after the Dead Rabbits Riot when Governor John King selected Daniel Conover for the post of Street Commissioner following the sudden death of the previous incumbent. On July 16, Conover arrived at City Hall as scheduled for his first day of work, fully expecting to be ushered into his new office, but instead he was greeted by surly Municipal police officers at the door. There must have been some miscommunication, said the officers as they barred him from entry. Mayor Wood, they explained, had decided to override the governor's appointment and had chosen to award the post to a highly successful contractor and bondsman named Charles Devlin, who previously ran for a seat on the Board of Aldermen. When the exasperated Conover attempted to push past the Municipals, he was brutishly escorted out of the premises. Undeterred, he secured a warrant for the mayor's arrest, which he aimed to enforce with the aid of the now-Metropolitan

Officer Walling. The city, Conover claimed, had reason to believe that Devlin had illegally purchased the position from Wood to the tune of $50,000 (approximately $1.4 million today).

Conover and Walling returned to City Hall, flashing their warrants, and demanded to be let in, but they were again refused entry by the 300 Municipals who had been preemptively stationed in the building. Presumably unaware of the size of the Municipal force, Walling revisited City Hall a few hours later with a piddling crew of 50 Metropolitan officers. The Municipals burst forth from City Hall and clashed with the Metropolitans, and for the next half hour or so, the brawling officers pushed, punched, and tore at each other's throats. 53 officers were hospitalized, and one patrolman surnamed Crofut was rendered immobile for the rest of his life.

Mayor Wood rebuffed the warrants and declined to leave the comfort of his office. Though he was eventually arrested, he was released on bail less than an hour later. Thanks to his connections, Wood was never tried, and the matter was buried shortly after the civil courts sided with him. Governor King, the court determined, had no legal say in mayoral appointments. A few months after the incident, now referred to as the "New York City Police Riot," or simply, "The Great Police Riot," the wounded Metropolitan officers slapped Wood with a series of lawsuits. Again, the seemingly untouchable Wood paid the suits no mind, and the city was left to reimburse the injured officers, who received $250 (about $6,000 today) each.

A depiction of the riot

Probes and Reforms

"Speak softly and carry a big stick – and you will go far." – President Theodore Roosevelt's advice to NYPD officers

For all its flaws, Tammany Hall played a pivotal role in reshaping the average New Yorkers' perception of the Irish, as well as immigrants in general. The employment of Irish policemen, officials, and statesmen began to climb, and soon became commonplace. Apart from Devlin, who immigrated to New York from Ireland at the age of 27, Tammany Hall head William "Boss" Tweed was succeeded by the devout Irish Catholic "Honest John" Kelly in 1872.

The new uniforms in 1871

In conjunction with those changes, the NYPD's disastrous early years were salvaged by the milestones they achieved towards the close of the 19th century. In 1882, authorities inaugurated the department's first-ever Detective Bureau, and in the autumn of 1887, a standard-issue pistol, a .32 double action four-inch barrel Colt revolver, was selected for NYPD officers for the first time. Four years later, the department hosted an induction ceremony for a quartet of police matrons – the first female staff members of the NYPD – who were brought on board to guard and transport female prisoners.

Although the department was improving, the criminality within the NYPD itself was no secret to everyday New Yorkers. The papers circulated sensational stories about the force's ineptitude and the political chicanery officers regularly engaged in. The public protested and called for change, and typically, the authorities responded with some vague and halfhearted promise to do better or orchestrated some other distraction that would entertain the forgetful masses. Once the scandal blew over, the public reverted to their previous state of indifference, where they remained until the next shocking headline.

In 1894, the Lexow Committee, the brainchild of New York Senator Clarence Lexow, attempted to break this toxic cycle by launching what was then the most comprehensive, state-funded inquiry into the NYPD. The anti-corruption task force was in large part inspired by the undercover operation that Reverend-Doctor Charles Henry Parkhurst conducted in the seedy underbelly of New York City two years prior. Parkhurst revealed his findings, backed by affidavits and other legitimate documentation, to a horrified congregation at the Madison Square Presbyterian Church. Tammany Hall and its Municipal force, Parkhurst thundered, were duplicitous, vice-indulgent plagues to society, "a lying, perjured, rum-soaked, and libidinous lot…While we fight iniquity, they shield and patronize it. While we try to convert criminals, they manufacture them."

Lexow

The probe uncovered the disconcerting depths of the department's malfeasance. Following up on Parkhurst's investigation, the committee published extensive reports detailing the department's involvement, as well as how they profited from prostitution, gambling arenas, and other vice-based enterprises. Corrupt cops brokered deals with counterfeiting rings, illegal saloons, gambling house operators, brothel proprietors, and pimps, and they looked the other way thanks to regular installments of hush money. Meanwhile, Tammany Hall profited from the city's bail system.

Promotions were not determined by performance evaluations or seniority, but the strength of bank accounts and political connections. Captain Timothy J. Creedon confessed to coughing up $15,000 (roughly $454,000 today) for his title. Purchasing the position, Creedon explained, was the last resort - he had been pining after the title for years, and was more than adequately qualified for the rank, pointing to the 97.82 he scored on the captain exam. He petitioned the Tammany boss of his district, John W. Reppenhagen, for the promotion based on his merit, but in response the official demanded $12,000 from him instead. Creedon returned to Reppenhagen's chambers a few weeks later with the $12,000 he had managed to pool together (with some assistance from local businesses), but by then, the price tag had swelled to $15,000 due to the heightened interest in the position. In a bid to prevent a prolonged bidding war, Creedon scrounged up another $3,000 and was guaranteed the title shortly thereafter.

Senior NYPD officials, the committee found, were also unscrupulously cashing in on the secret quid pro quo relationships they harbored with dishonest businessmen and other affluent members of the New York elite. Irish Superintendent (Police Chief) Thomas F. Byrnes revealed that his personal net worth amounted to $350,000, approximately $10.6 million today, and he credited railroad and shipping tycoon Cornelius Vanderbilt and fellow railroad magnate Jay Gould with funding the better part of his astonishing wealth. In exchange for these "gifts," Byrnes and his men staved off anti-capitalist and labor activists, disbanded the strikes of disgruntled employees, and remained at the beck and call of their employers all 365 days of the year.

The Lexow Committee was among the first of many exhaustive investigations launched against the department throughout the chaotic, but riveting history of the NYPD. The testimonies derived from the investigative hearings were compiled into a rambling document that ran over 10,000 pages long, and one journalist referred to the feat as "the most detailed accounting of municipal malfeasance in history." The committee's findings helped ensure the victory of the Republican candidate, William L. Strong, in the 1894 mayoral elections. Strong was endorsed by the Committee of Seventy, a separate task force originally formed in 1871 to investigate the alleged embezzlement and other crimes of Tammany Hall's Boss Tweed.

Strong

A year after the formation of the Lexow Committee, the newly-elected Strong fired all the members of the four-member panel that previously oversaw the police department and replaced them with fresh blood. An up-and-coming statesman, Theodore Roosevelt, was appointed President of the new NYPD Police Commission. A passionate crusader at heart, Roosevelt, sworn in on May 6, 1895, pledged to flush out all the evils within the department once and for all.

Partisanship was strictly forbidden in Roosevelt's department. Relying on his knowledge of meritocracy from his time with the Civil Service, Roosevelt applied this fairness to the police department, with his reach extending well beyond the law. As Police Commissioner, Roosevelt was also intimately involved with the New York Board of Health. To assist his Health duties, Roosevelt met Jacob Riis, the renowned photographer and author of *How the Other Half Lives.* Together, the two toured some of New York's poorest tenements and neighborhoods. Of the experience, Roosevelt later wrote, "It is one thing to listen in perfunctory fashion to tales of overcrowded tenements, and it is quite another actually to see what that overcrowding means."

Commissioner Roosevelt

Jacob Riis

The Riis-Roosevelt partnership helped crystalize what was to become the Roosevelt legacy of ardent progressivism. He took on wealthy tenement owners, who insisted that it was unconstitutional to tell them to provide better conditions for their renters. For Roosevelt, such moneyed interests saw the Constitution "not as a help to righteousness, but as a means for thwarting movements against unrighteousness." His time as Police Commissioner solidified Roosevelt's life-long transition from wealthy aristocrat to man of the people.

Roosevelt was literally not one to sleep on the job, as exemplified by a sting he and Riis conducted one night in June 1895. A little after midnight, the self-appointed sleuths slipped into the eerily silent streets, and for the next few hours they tailed and observed the activities of the oblivious policemen from afar. On June 8, the *New York Times* published a story describing their observations. In the article, entitled, "Police Caught Napping," Riis and Roosevelt claimed to have found cops snoozing behind their desks and in their police wagons, while other officers on duty were caught boozing in nondescript saloons and messing around in pool halls.

Roosevelt restated his disappointment with the underperforming patrolmen and their complacent superiors and urged them to strive for excellence. The ideal police officer, according to Roosevelt, possessed the following qualities: "The credit belongs to the man who is actually in the arena; whose face is marred by dust, sweat and blood; who strives valiantly; who errs and comes short again and again; who knows great enthusiasms, the great devotions, and spends himself in a worthy cause; who at best knows in the end the triumph of high achievement; and at worst, if he fails, at least fails while daring greatly..."

Roosevelt held the post for just two years, but the reforms he implemented and attempted to implement would stand the test of time. To start with, Roosevelt made entrance and promotional exams across all ranks mandatory. He erected an obstacle course, kitted out with a shooting range, which chroniclers believe partially prompted the creation of standard police academies.

Among Roosevelt's most significant innovations was the establishment of the NYPD Bicycle Squad in December of 1895, otherwise referred to as the "Scorcher Squad," to ameliorate the city's traffic safety issues. Pedestrians and safe drivers who adhered to the road rules were living in fear of the multiplying speed fiends who blatantly ignored the speed limit. The Scorcher Squad, Roosevelt hoped, would restore order to the streets. Scorcher officers pedaled to their respective booths, scattered around the city's busiest thoroughfares, where they dutifully logged the speeds of all passing vehicles. Whenever a vehicle was caught speeding, the patrolman rung up the upcoming booth in the offending vehicle's path. Upon receiving that call, the officer stationed at the next booth would either intercept or give chase to the suspect.

The department achieved more notable firsts during Roosevelt's brief tenure. In 1896, the NYPD welcomed George Garcia to the force, making him the first Hispanic officer of the department. A year prior to Garcia's appointment, Minnie Gertrude Kelly was named Secretary of the Police Commission, becoming the first-ever woman to work at the NYPD headquarters.

By the end of his tenure with the New York Police Department, Roosevelt was quickly becoming a household name. What was once the most corrupt and ineffective law enforcement agency in the nation had transitioned into an example of a police force that worked for the common good. The city's police were held to higher standards; Roosevelt made sure they were actually patrolling when they were supposed to be, a common problem before his tenure. And police hostels which had housed policeman while they were supposedly "on duty" were closed. Roosevelt's strictness and tough policies ensured that the nation's fastest growing city was no longer ridden with crime and insecurity.

That said, despite Roosevelt's best efforts, it would never be possible to undo decades worth of corruption. As Richard Zacks, author of *Island of Vice: Theodore Roosevelt's Doomed Quest to Clean Up Sin-Loving New York*, put it, "In hindsight, what [Roosevelt] was trying to do, it's like somebody going into Vegas and just saying, 'there's gonna be no more gambling.'"

This was made clear on January 1, 1898, when the Bronx, Brooklyn, Queens, Staten Island, and Manhattan were all absorbed into New York City. With that, the five boroughs' 18 police departments were merged into one, resulting in a consolidated force of close to 7,000 officers. Grand Sachem of Tammany Hall Richard Croker bent over backwards to ensure that the posts of Chief of Police and Superintendent of the Police Commission were guaranteed to disgraced Police Captain William "Big Bill" Devery, the future co-owner of the New York Yankees.

Devery

Croker

The public was well-aware of the Devery family's long-time association with the Democrats, but it was not the favoritism, which they had grown accustomed to, that bothered them. It was that Devery had been expelled from the force about a year earlier after being charged with bribery and extortion. His conviction was eventually overturned, and he was reinstated to the force as a lowly inspector just a week after the concurrent expansion of New York City and the NYPD. Be that as it may, his vindication in court did nothing to sway the jaded members of the public who had absolutely no faith in the justice system.

They were even less impressed by Croker's shameless manipulation of the system. Normally, Devery's middling title would have rendered him ineligible for the premier position of Superintendent. Following a calculated sequence of string-pulling and loophole-finding, however, Croker had Devery named Deputy Chief on February 14 and set in motion the conveniently timed retirement of John McCullagh that spring. Devery was bumped up to Superintendent of the four-member board on June 30.

Croker and Devery's takeover of the New York Police Department antagonized reform activists across the state. Three months later, *Harper's Weekly* published a feature piece entitled "Wide-Open New York," which explored Croker and Devery's antics and the comeback of widespread police corruption. The gripping exposé, penned by journalist Franklin Matthews, explained the extortion tactics of Tammany Hall politicians and NYPD officers in further detail, their involvement in the illegal prize-fighting scene, and their intentional disregard for state-issued liquor and vice laws. The same article accused the disreputable politicians and policemen of election fraud, voter intimidation, and fraternizing with counterfeiting rings. Devery, as maintained by the unidentified officers interviewed for the article, warned his men, "When you're caught with the goods on, just don't say nothin'."

THE BIG CHIEF'S FAIRY GODMOTHER
Mr. Devery tells " where he got it "

A satirical cartoon of Devery

A follow-up article published by *The New York Times* alleged that NYPD and Tammany Hall heads received over $3 million (a dizzying $79.36 million today) in protection fees each year from a single gambling den alone.

In the early months of 1899, Governor Theodore Roosevelt worked with other Republican lawmakers to form another investigative committee, this time chaired by Robert Mazet. The investigation would focus on the leaders of Tammany Hall, and Devery was called in for questioning in April of that year. Unbeknownst to Devery, committee-commissioned detectives had been watching him like a hawk in the weeks leading up to the interrogation. They discovered that he regularly left his office about 7:00 p.m. to stand guard at the intersection between 8th Avenue and 21st Street, where he supposedly serviced anyone that sought his assistance until

2:00 a.m. Despite his purported familiarity with the area, Devery claimed to have no knowledge of the illegal saloon directly across the street.

In October 1900, *Harper's Weekly* contributor Franklin Matthews released the second installment of the Tammany Hall and NYPD exposé under the theatrical title, "The Cost of Tammany Hall in Flesh and Blood." Matthews called attention to the upsurge in the rates and intensity of juvenile crimes, which he attributed to the apathy and ineffectiveness of NYPD officers. He placed great emphasis on the state's worrying death rates, the leading causes being homicides and unsanitary, hazardous living conditions, and called for the self-congratulatory politicians to take responsibility for their negligence. Matthews also shined a light on how women, children, and other vulnerable members of society were suffering as a result of the broken system.

Towards the final months of Roosevelt's stint as governor, he signed a document authorizing the dissolution of the four-man committee that presided over the NYPD, as well as the redundant title of "Chief of Police." From that point forward, control over the city police department lay in the hands of a single Police Commissioner. Upon the discontinuation of the once-coveted positions of Board Superintendent and Police Chief, the now-jobless Devery was demoted to Chief Inspector, and when Michael C. Murphy replaced him as the department's sole Police Commissioner in 1901, Devery was given the title of Deputy Commissioner. Unfortunately for Devery, he was never afforded the opportunity to settle into his new titles, for his Tammany Hall supporters lost the mayoral election to the Republican candidate, Seth Low, that November.

The 20th Century

"I have my own army in the NYPD, which is the seventh biggest army in the world..." – New York City Mayor Michael Bloomberg

The premiere of epoch-making scientific discoveries and transformative technological advancements at the start of the 20th century kindled a golden age of sorts within the NYPD. A rudimentary crew composed of explosives experts was unofficially established in the fall of 1905 in response to the spike in improvised explosive device attacks, mainly employed by Italian "Black Hand" gangs as a part of their terror campaigns. Padula-born NYPD Officer Joe Petrosino and his so-called "Italian Squad" were tasked with shadowing Black Hand members and predicting the settings of the next attacks. Petrosino continued to spearhead that task force until he was killed on a mission abroad in 1909.

The task force adjourned shortly after Petrosino's death, but it was resurrected five years later. Inspector Thomas J. Tunney was selected to captain the new crew of explosives specialists, aptly rechristened the "Bomb Squad," which consisted of what was left of Petrosino's Italian Squad and other new recruits. *Standing Well Back*, a blog dedicated to historical and modern explosives, summed up Tunney's tenure: "Tunney's job initially was to continue the focus on

Italian and mafia extortion gangs using IEDs, and the continuing anarchist revolutionary threat – and the emerging threat from German saboteurs. Tunney coordinated a significant effort from his team of 34 detectives, and led the use of double agents and detectives working undercover, as well as extensive surveillance operations...His team [later] prevented an attack on St. Patrick's Cathedral by some anarchists in 1915, when the bomb planters were arrested 'in the act' by undercover police officers, one of whom pulled the fuse from the IED to prevent the explosion."

Two years after the introduction of Petrosino's Bomb Squad, Police Commissioner Theodore A. Bingham launched what is now called the "Purge," or "Slaughter of April 1907." The title of Police Commissioner, Bingham complained, bore far less weight than the elegance of the position suggests. He was unable to properly exercise his authority over the high-ranking officials of the department, specifically the Inspectors, who remained loyal only to the politicians who awarded them their posts. The depravity poisoning the department, Bingham concluded, stemmed from these very Inspectors.

The media echoed Bingham's concerns. One article complained, "Commissioners come and go every four years or less. But the cabal of Inspectors who make the system goes on forever, bending captains and sergeants to its will by reasons of the long tenure of the men who administer the system, and the pressure which they can exert without knowledge of the Commissioner."

In addition to the eight Inspectors and "unnumbered" Detective Sergeants expelled by the purge, backed by Governor Charles Evan Hughes, Bingham retired superfluous titles and created new posts. Several officers were affected, both positively and negatively, by his restructuring of the hierarchy. Most of the Inspectors who made the cut were demoted to Captains, their former subordinates. The surviving Detective Sergeants, rebranded as "Lieutenants," were extracted from the Detective Bureau and dispersed across various departments throughout the state. Furthermore, all commanding officers, who previously presided over at least two adjoining precincts, were now placed in charge of just one precinct.

One of the three orders in the Bingham Bill listed the new and modified titles, as well as the fixed salaries of each post, as follows: "Inspectors - \$3,500; Captain - \$2,750; Lieutenants - \$2,000; Sergeants - \$1,500; 1st Grade Patrolman - \$1,400; 2nd Grade Patrolman - \$1,350; 3rd Grade Patrolman - \$1,250; 4th Grade Patrolman - \$1,150; 5th Grade Patrolman - \$1,000; and finally, 6th Grade Patrolman - \$900."

On June 9, 1911, Police Commissioner Waldo Rhinelander introduced the "Motorcycle Squad," a division of the Office of Street Traffic Regulation Bureau. The new traffic force debuted their glinting collection of 25 cherry-red "Indian" motorcycles a week later. The Motorcycle Squad was the next step in the evolution of the Bicycle Squad, which could no longer outpace the now mass-produced motorized automobiles. It did not take long for the new division to prove its worth. Between June 9 and December 31st of 1911, the Motorcycle Squad issued a total of 3,710 speeding tickets amounting to $17,816 (approximately $407,000 today).

On June 28 of the same year, the NYPD welcomed its first African-American officer, Samuel J. Battle. Rhinelander, who played master of ceremony at Battle's induction, was proud of the recruit's achievements, but he recognized the arduous uphill climb that lay ahead. Shortly after the recital of the oath, he told Battle, "You will have some difficulties ahead of you, but I am certain you will overcome them."

More landmark moments followed suit. In 1912, Isabella Goodwin, a native of Greenwich Village known for solving a Manhattan robbery that stumped the 60-something detectives assigned to the case, made history when she was named the first female "first grade" detective of the NYPD. Even so, the term "policewoman" was only officially integrated into department speak in 1918, upon the induction of a batch of six female police officers. Two years later, Lawon R. Bruce, the first female African-American police officer, was sworn into the force.

Unfortunately, whatever positive publicity the New York Police Department managed to conjure up in the early years of the 20th century was besmirched in the second half of the 20th century. The 1960s is often romanticized as a delightfully progressive, inclusive era defined by peace and free love, but New Yorkers and other Americans in the LGBTQ community, regrettably, were not entitled to this "free love." Same-sex relationships and relations were outlawed by the New York courts. Similarly, public displays of affection and dressing in drag were prohibited and categorized as "gross indecency and lewdness." Those who violated these laws were either arrested or subjected to severe beatings with billy clubs.

When John Lindsay was elected mayor in 1965, the Mattachine Society was able to persuade him to end much of the police harassment that had been aimed at the gay community up to that time. However, authorities continued to target bars that were known to serve gay customers.

Lindsay

LGBTQ and non-binary New Yorkers sought refuge in underground gay bars and disco halls. These were safe spaces, where they could theoretically be free of judgment and violence. One of the most popular gay bars in New York was the Stonewall Inn, located on Christopher Street in Greenwich Village. Like other similar establishments, it was owned and run by a mafia family, in this case the Genovese family. About a week after the infamous raid on the Stonewall, an article in *The New York Daily News* described the Stonewall as "a two-story structure with a sand painted brick and opaque glass facade…a mecca for the homosexual element in the village who wanted nothing but a private little place where they could congregate, drink, dance and do whatever little girls do when they get together…The thick glass shut out the outside world of the street. Inside, the Stonewall bathed in wild, bright psychedelic lights, while the patrons writhed to the sounds of a juke box on a square dance floor surrounded by booths and tables. The bar did a good business and the waiters, or waitresses, were always kept busy, as they snaked their way around the dancing customers to the booths and tables. For nearly two years, peace and tranquility reigned supreme for the Alice in Wonderland clientele."

The Stonewall Inn, courtesy of the New York Public Library

Like other gay establishments, the Stonewall had its own methods for appearing to be legitimate. Martin Boyce, who lived in Greenwich Village at the time, noted that "in the front part of the bar would be like 'A' gays, like regular gays, that didn't go in any kind of drag, didn't use the word 'she,' that type, but they were gay, a hundred percent gay. And then as you turned into the other room with the jukebox, those were the drag queens around the jukebox."

Since the Stonewall was the only gay bar in New York City that allowed dancing, its owners had a special system to avoid being raided. If the police were suspected to be near the place, the lights on the dance floor change color, letting everyone know that they should separate. Meanwhile, a separate room at the back of the bar catered to transgendered people.

The authorities' undue obsession with the rainbow community, however, led to their discovery of the underground network of LGBTQ-friendly pubs. The New York State Liquor Authority ordered the immediate shutdown of the rainbow safe havens and imposed hefty fines on the proprietors of "straight" establishments that were caught serving alcohol to "known or suspected LGBT individuals."

In 1966, the alcohol ban imposed on LGBTQ individuals was lifted, but expressing one's love for the same sex in any way, shape, or form continued to be illegal. The NYPD were no longer vested with the power to prevent members of the community from enjoying a simple nightcap, so long as the bar was equipped with the proper paperwork. Even so, officers continued to storm into LGBTQ havens and other allied bars unannounced, rifling through the stock for illicit liquor stashes, rounding up patrons who were much too intimate for their liking and searching for other creative ways to persecute those who lived their lives against the norm.

Raids were frequent and typically followed the same pattern. Police officer Seymour Pine later explained, "We'd go in, and the first police officer that went in with your group went to the bartender, flashed his shield and [announced], 'The place is under arrest. When you exit have some ID and it'll be over in a short time.' And that was it. It would take maybe a half hour to clear the place out.' … I was in charge of five precincts that had to do with public morals: gambling, prostitution, liquor, social crimes, [all things] that should not have been part of the police department. But that was the way it was set up. … It made you feel lousy really, because most of them were school kids or those who had just recently gotten out of school. It made you feel like you were spoiling [whatever] fun they had. … I felt badly for those people who were being arrested and who foolishly gave their right names. These kids had no idea that if they got arrested for this, then they couldn't pass the bar and they couldn't be in a lot of professions, because they had a criminal record."

Tensions between the NYPD and LGBTQ New Yorkers came to a head on June 28, 1969, when a unit of NYPD officers, consisting of four plainclothes policemen, a pair of patrolmen, one detective, and a deputy inspector, swooped into the Stonewall. The cops, flashing their warrants, strutted about the premises, callously manhandling both employees and customers, and raiding the back room for bootlegged booze. 13 were arrested, among them employees deemed insufficiently cooperative and innocent cross-dressers and drag queens found violating the state's ordinance regarding gender-appropriate attire. A few other patrons suspected of gender-bending were dragged into the bathroom, where waiting female officers performed supremely invasive exams. Among those patted down and violently frisked was a then pre-operative transgender woman named Maria Ritter, who recalled, "My biggest fear was that I would get arrested. My second biggest fear was that my picture would be in a newspaper or on a television report in my mother's dress."

Faced with opposition, the police decided to take everyone into custody and called for patrol wagons to transport them. However, as they gathered together the patrons, they soon realized that they were badly outnumbered. As is often the case in such situations, a crowd was beginning to gather outside as word spread that something was going on down at the Stonewall, and some Greenwich Village residents were understandably outraged by the raid and the NYPD's abhorrent treatment of the Stonewall's staff and customers. A buzzing mob of between 100-150 congregated around the Stonewall entrance as the officers and their captives awaited the police vehicles that were scheduled to pick up the 28 cases of beer and 19 bottles of hard liquor that were confiscated.

At first, the impromptu demonstrators attempted to kill the officers with kindness, breaking into spirited chants of "Gay power!" They also broke into song, many opting for the motivational anthem "We Shall Overcome." That said, the atmosphere darkened at once when the irritated officers began to hassle the arrested in plain view of the crowd. The pot bubbled over when a cop struck one of the protesters, a lesbian referred to as a "typical dyke-stone butch," with his nightstick in an effort to subdue and arrest her. As she was thrust into the back of a cop car, she turned towards her fellow protesters and called upon the crowd to take action. The crowd reacted, hurling pennies, bottles, pebbles, and other projectiles within reach at the panicking cops.

According to Lucian Truscott, IV, a reporter for *The Village Voice*, "Suddenly the paddywagon arrived and the mood of the crowd changed. Three of the more blatant queens -- in full drag -- were loaded inside, along with the bartender and doorman, to a chorus of catcalls and boos from the crowd. A cry went up to push the paddywagon over, but it drove away before anything could happen. With its exit, the action waned momentarily. The next person to come out was a dyke, and she put up a struggle -- from car to door to car again. It was at that moment that the scene became explosive…Beer cans and bottles were heaved at the windows, and a rain of coins descended on the cops."

Unable to fend off the growing mob and unfolding riot, the police, along with Truscott, ducked into the bar and sealed off the doors. When those inside the bar refused to capitulate, members of the mob shattered the windows with bricks, lit pieces of trash ablaze, flung them into the windows, and squirted lighter fluid on the floors. Fortunately, the flames were eventually extinguished by the fire department, and the crowd was dispersed by the riot squad, who arrived to the scene shortly thereafter. The unrest, marked by more violent protests (and some peaceful demonstrations) and skirmishes with the cops, continued to rage on for the next five days.

The Stonewall Riots, also referred to as "The Stonewall Uprising," offered tangible proof of the authorities' prejudice towards the LGBTQ community. The uprising propelled the gay rights movement in New York, as well as in the United States, to the next level. A year after the Stonewall ordeal, LGBTQ residents and allies paraded up and down Christopher Street and Sixth Avenue, making it the state's first LGBTQ pride march. Ironically, a few of the police officers who were present at Stonewall were tasked with guarding the very same protesters they had been wrangling into paddy wagons just a year earlier.

The department name suffered another debilitating blow during the outbreak of the crack cocaine epidemic in the late 1980s and early 1990s. New Yorkers were first introduced to the drug in 1985, not long after cocaine manufacturers in Los Angeles mastered the art of converting pricey powdered cocaine into cheap, rock-like pellets. Jay Maeder, author of *Big Town, Big Time: A New York Epic (1898-1998)*, described the highly destructive effects of the drug: "Perversely, crack packed an even bigger wallop than cocaine, and caused the typical user to become addicted much faster. Crack vapor got to the brain in about five seconds. The euphoric rush would last just about 10 minutes, and then the user would be overwhelmed by a depression erasable only by another hit on the crack pipe."

The uncontainable crack craze reached new heights in 1988, and homicide statistics were the worst they had ever been in years. Close to 40% of the 1,896 homicides recorded that year were attributed to drugs, and impoverished neighborhoods suffered inordinately from the epidemic. There was a sharp uptick in violent crime in the South Bronx, a 44% increase from 1985. Thomas Reppetto, president of the Citizens Crime Commission, complained, "Crack crime in poor neighborhoods [was] at such levels that if the same were true in wealthy neighborhoods, we would be under martial law."

The NYPD was rebuked for their inability to tame the crack craze and the resulting territorial wars. Many pointed to "Baby" Sam Edmonson, a kingpin who raked in an average of $100,000 a day and was blamed for at least nine deaths within an 18-month period.

Meanwhile, the city was still struggling to recover from the 1970s fiscal crisis, which cut manufacturing jobs in half and hurt the NYPD's finances. By 1990, the department's roster had plummeted from 42,000 to about 27,000. The shortage of NYPD officers was especially troubling, as a record-breaking 2,245 homicides were recorded that same year.

The department's reputation continued to deteriorate in the 1990s. In September 1992, David Dinkins, the city's first African-American mayor, proposed that NYPD representatives be dismissed from committees formed to investigate police misconduct. This did not sit well with the majority white force and its union, and in response, about 10,000 off-duty NYPD officers flooded Brooklyn Bridge, ignored the deafening honks of the congested cars, and headed for City Hall Park. As they scaled the steps of the governmental building, the officers chanted, "Dinkins must go!" *Newsday* equated City Hall with an "embassy in some far-off hostile land...under siege." The *New York Times* called the boisterous gathering a "beer-swilling, traffic-snarling, epithet-hurling melee."

A 2016 *Guardian* article described the demonstration and the ensuing aftermath in further detail: "The signs the police waved labeled the mayor a 'washroom attendant,' claimed he was 'on crack,' said his 'true color was yellow-bellied,' and asked if he had hugged a drug dealer that day. A subsequent official NYPD report, which recommended discipline for 42 officers and called the march an 'embarrassment,' conceded some protesters used racial slurs and said the rally was 'unruly, mean-spirited, and perhaps criminal.'"

Dinkins

The NYPD Today

It took an unthinkable tragedy of catastrophic proportions to give the department's reputation the boost it urgently needed.

Intelligence experts now believe that al-Qaeda began to put the 9/11 plot into motion around 1999, following a series of meetings in 1999 between Osama bin Laden and Khalid Sheikh Mohammad that likely discussed the attacks. Another member of al-Qaeda, Mohammed Atef, began planning the logistics of the attack, including coordinating travel for the hijackers. Some leaders from al-Qaeda reported that bin Laden himself chose the targets for the attack. It's believed that some of the initial targets were the U.S. Capitol, the White House, and the World Trade Center.

In the early summer of 2000, an additional group of terrorists from Hamburg arrived in the United States to begin flight training. The men included Mohamed Atta, Marwan al-Shehhi, and Ziad Jarrah. This group of men, along with Hanjour, would operate the airplanes after hijacking them. In conjunction with these pilots, al-Qaeda began to select muscle hijackers around the summer of 2000. This second group of terrorists would force the cockpit and airplane crew to rescind power of the airplanes can control passengers. Despite the fact the phrase "muscle hijackers" was widely used to describe these men and their roles in the attacks, most of them were only between 5' 5" and 5' 7" tall.

When al-Hazmi and al-Mihdhar arrived in the U.S. in early 2000, it quickly became clear to al-Qaeda just how difficult an operation 9/11 was going to be. After landing in Los Angeles, the two men began taking flying lessons in San Diego, with al-Qaeda intentionally choosing locations in California because it was an easy entry point from Asia and far removed from the intended targets on the East Coast. Both men had planned to learn English and learn to fly, possibly to receive pilot licenses, but they quickly set off red flags with their flight instructors. The two men started flight school completely inexperienced with piloting, but they immediately explained to their flight instructors that they were interested in flying jets and did not want to train on small planes. Neither of the men were successful in obtaining pilot licenses, and al-Mihdhar left the United States after less than one year in the country.

Before al-Mihdhar's had even left the country, al-Qaeda leaders had determined that additional operatives were needed in the United States and began to plan for the possibility that one or both of the operatives currently in the United States would fail. As a result, al-Qaeda recruited four more men who would go to Afghanistan and undergo the same intensive training that the first four had received. The new operatives, consisting of Atta, Ramzi Binalshibh, Marwan al-Shehhi, and Ziad Jarrah, hailed from Egypt, United Arab Emirates, Lebanon and Yemen, but they had studied together in Hamburg, Germany, and all four had planned to use their skills to commit jihad in other parts of the world before being selected for the 9/11 attacks. These men were likely selected because they were educated, had experience living in Western society, were proficient in English, and would be more likely to obtain visas. In essence, they were likely to avoid the pitfalls that al-Qaeda believed would plague or had already plagued al-Mihdhar and al-Hazmi.

During the summer of 2001 the pilots kept busy by assisting the muscle hijackers and taking additional flight training, including cross-country flights. During training, two of the pilots requested that they be allowed to fly the Hudson Corridor, a low altitude flight along the Hudson River that passed by the World Trade Center. Al-Shehhi took a cross-country trip from New York to San Francisco on May 24, and others took similar flights following Shehhi. The purpose of the cross-country flights was to determine what obstacles the men might encounter on the day of the attacks, with each man flying first class in the same type of plane he would later pilot.

Immediately preceding the attacks, top al-Qaeda officials met in Spain to plan the final details of the attack. Some reports indicate that there was some disagreement between al-Qaeda and the Taliban about how the attacks should be implemented. Regardless, by early 2001, United States officials were beginning to receive frequent reports about threats from Al-Qaeda, and during the summer of 2001, more and more threats poured in. Many officials recognized the summer of 2001 as unprecedented for the number of threat reports, which suggested an imminent attack. However, many reports were fragmented or unclear, and intelligence officials were unprepared for the type of attack al-Qaeda was planning, as it had never been attempted by a terrorist group before.

Oddly enough, as horrific as the subsequent attacks were, the scenario itself was not completely unanticipated. The Port Authority of New York and New Jersey had previously hosted a drill involving such a scenario at the World Trade Center on November 7, 1982. Port Authority officers aside, members of the NYPD, the New York City Fire Department, and the Emergency Medical Services took part in the training exercise. Director of the Port Authority's World Trade Department, Guy Tozzoli, provided the specifics of the drill at a legislative hearing held on March 29th, 1993. As reported by *History Commons*, "[Tozzoli] recalled that the Port Authority simulated the 'total disaster' of 'the airplane hitting the building' and participants simulated 'blood coming out of the people.' He [added] that the drill was 'a real preparation for a disaster.' The drill [followed] an incident in 1981, when an Argentine aircraft came within 90 seconds of crashing into the World Trade Center's North Tower as a result of having problems communicating with air traffic controllers...The 1982 exercise appears to be the last 'joint drill involving all the emergency responders' held at the WTC prior to the 9/11 attacks."

The influx of threats declined significantly in August, and the threats were all but non-existent in early September, signifying the calm before the storm. After 9/11, the 9/11 Commission Report demonstrated the disturbing ease with which the hijackers entered the country and freely moved around, as well as other clues about their intentions while at flight school. For example, all of the 9/11 hijackers entered the country legally using their real names, and even though all of the hijackers had likely traveled to Afghanistan at one time or another for training, the hijackers were easily able to conceal this by traveling through Iran (which did not stamp Saudi passports) or by having their passports doctored by al-Qaeda experts. Furthermore, the eventual hijacker pilots attended flight school under their real names, and some of them had demonstrated no interest in learning how to land or take off. The 9/11 Commission's Report also stated that the

Mossad, Israel's intelligence agency, gave Atta's name to the CIA on August 23, 2001 as part of a list of names believed to be planning an imminent attack. Al-Shehhi, al-Mihdhar and al-Hazmi were also on the list.

In the weeks before 9/11, the 19 terrorists began making their last-minute preparations inside the U.S. Some of the men continued to practice flying rented planes, while others trained at gyms in hotels where they were staying. The operatives also purchased multiple knives, which they likely planned to use during the attacks. During the last week of August, one of the men purchased a GPS unit from a pilot shop in Miami, along with aeronautical charts. However, none of these activities or purchases raised any suspicions. Unlike other terrorist attacks, where the men would have to buy bomb-making materials, these purchases were seen as typical.

Approximately two weeks before the attacks, the men began purchasing plane tickets on the planes they would eventually hijack. The training provided by Khalid Sheikh Mohammed was put to use, as the operatives purchased the tickets at airports, on the phone and by Internet. They then wired their excess funds back to al-Qaeda, totaling about $26,000. Experts estimate that in all, al-Qaeda spent approximately $500,000 on the attacks, with approximately half of that money being spent in the United States.

Finally, the terrorists traveled to the departure points where they would board planes on 9/11. The men who eventually hijacked American Airlines Flight 77 grouped in Laurel, Maryland, staying at a motel there during the first week of September and even spending time at a neighboring gym. The night before the attacks, they stayed at a hotel in Herndon, Virginia, closer to the airport. Meanwhile, the men who would hijack United Airlines Flight 93 stayed in Newark. The group that hijacked United Airlines Flight 175 arrived in Boston. Only Atta and another member of his group would take a connecting flight on 9/11 itself, traveling from Portland, Maine before boarding American Airlines Flight 11.

September 11, 2001 started as a typical Tuesday morning in New York City, with clear skies. People were still heading to work across Manhattan, including taking trains to the World Trade Center. At 8:46 a.m., people on the streets heard the throttle of a passenger jet overhead but had no reason to pay any attention to it until they heard an extremely loud explosion. The first hijacked plane, American Airlines Flight 11, had just struck the North Tower of the World Trade Center.

Immediately after the first plane hit the North Tower, before it was even clear what had happened, both buildings began to be evacuated. However, on the floors above the plane's impact, no one could evacuate because the plane's impact had destroyed all three emergency stairwells. With smoke and fire spreading, many of the people trapped in the North Tower headed toward windows.

Less than two minutes after the crash, a news crew which had been reporting on the mayoral primary elections for WNYW broadcast the first pictures of the crash. The reporter, Dick Oliver, informed viewers:

"Jim, just a few moments ago something believed to be a plane crashed into the South Tower of the World Trade Center. I just saw flames inside. You can see the smoke coming out of the tower. We have no idea what it was. It was a tremendous boom just a few moments ago. You can hear around me emergency vehicles heading towards the scene. Now this could have been an aircraft or it could have been something internal. It appears to be something coming from the outside, due the nature of the opening on about the 100th floor of the South Tower of the World Trade Center." The reporter, Oliver, had mistaken the South Tower for the North Tower and later corrected himself.

Initial media reports were confused about whether a plane had hit the World Trade Center or whether the explosion occurred internally, but some witnesses claimed to have seen a plane hit the North Tower. CNN broke into a commercial with the headline "World Trade Center disaster", a live shot of the North Tower on fire, and no further information.

Firefighters began to arrive at the World Trade Center by 8:50 a.m. and set up a command post in the lobby of the North Tower. From there, firefighters and other personnel were sent up into the North Tower to find people and evacuate the building. At 9:00 a.m., the chief of the New York Fire Department, Peter Ganci, arrived and ordered that the command post be moved across the street due to falling debris.

The first responders were also hampered by damage done to the North Tower's emergency repeater system, which was required for first responders' radio sets to work correctly. Due to the ongoing fire in the tower, the system malfunctioned, leaving firefighters unable to communicate with the command post or coordinate their actions with other firefighters or the police department.

First responders and other authorities began arriving at the World Trade Center within five minutes of Flight 11 hitting the North Tower, allowing rescue efforts to begin almost immediately. At first, the focus was on evacuating the floors immediately above and below the fires, which was the FDNY's standard procedure in a high-rise fire. However, firefighters soon determined that all three evacuation stairwells were blocked by the fires raging in the impact zone, and that those above the impact of the plane were trapped. Evacuating people by helicopter from the top of the towers was also impossible for a variety of reasons.

In the South Tower, a building-wide announcement was made on the public address system at 8:55 a.m., calling the building "secure" and advising occupants to go back to their offices. Many occupants of the South Tower had already evacuated, and others who could obviously see something was terribly wrong ignored the announcement and evacuated anyway. In particular, Morgan Stanley's security officer, Rick Rescoria, a Vietnam War veteran, ignored the building authorities and evacuated Morgan Stanley's offices anyway. When the second plane hit the South Tower, Morgan Stanley was already mostly evacuated. Of its 2,700 employees at work in the South Tower on 9/11, only six died. Four of those six were Rescoria and three deputies, who returned to the South Tower after evacuating to assist in evacuating others from the building.

In the North Tower, firefighters, NYPD officers, Port Authority officers and emergency medical technicians were all attempting to evacuate building occupants; however, their efforts were hampered by their radio systems, which were incompatible with each other. As a result, each agency duplicated the efforts of the others, meaning that some offices were checked as many as four times for occupants.

Of all the horrific images captured during the morning of September 11, 2001, few were as spellbinding or gut-wrenching as the live footage of United Airlines Flight 175 slamming into the South Tower. When American Airlines Flight 11 slammed into the North Tower at 8:46 a.m., it was initially thought a plane may have accidentally crashed into it, and many New Yorkers were familiar with a similar accident involving the Empire State Building several decades earlier. However, as national media outlets started carrying live footage of the damaged North Tower and began speculating as to what happened, they caught Flight 175 directly approaching the South Tower and slamming straight into it at 9:03 a.m.

By 9:51 a.m., nearly an hour after Flight 175 had crashed into the South Tower, FDNY firefighters had managed to get to the impact zone in the South Tower. Leading this team of firefighters were Battalion Chief Orio Palmer and Fire Marshall Ronald Bucca. Both took the last working elevator to the 44th floor and raced up the last 34 flights to get to the impact zone. At the time, Palmer, Bucca, and other firefighters were unaware of warnings called in by those stranded at the top the South Tower. Several 911 callers reported the 105th and 106th floors were collapsing, and police helicopters radioed that the South Tower appeared unstable from above. Although the firefighters had no idea about the South Tower's instability, these warnings did reach NYPD officers and Port Authority officers, and many of them evacuated the South Tower.

Immediately after the collapse of the South Tower, NYPD and other first responders other than firefighters pulled back from the North Tower as well. Although radio commands were given to pull back from the North Tower by commanders, most firefighters in the North Tower never received the order. The commands were radioed at least twice, but most firefighters never heard them due to the failing radio repeater system in the building. Furthermore, dust and smoke likely obscured any view of the South Tower's collapse by firefighters in the North Tower. As a result, most firefighters killed in the North Tower, like Palmer and Bucca in the South Tower, were unaware that they were running out of time. The total collapse of a high-rise was not usually considered in firefighter training; the strategy in high-rise fires was to evacuate people or move them to safe floors and then try to control the fire.

At 10:28 a.m., the North Tower collapsed, 100 minutes after Flight 11 hit it. The emergency stairwells that were to be used to evacuate the North Tower had been destroyed by the impact of the plane, so no one above the impact zone in the North Tower survived the attack.

Shortly after the second hijacked plane hit the South Tower, when it was apparent that New York City was suffering terrorist attacks, all bridges and tunnels into Manhattan were closed, literally leaving everyone on the island stranded. Most high-profile buildings and high rise buildings in New York City and elsewhere were also being evacuated, including the United Nations, the Empire State Building, the Sears Tower in Chicago, the Mall of America near Minneapolis, and the U.S. Bank Tower in Los Angeles.

Naturally, in New York City the evacuation included most of the buildings in Lower Manhattan. The NYPD determined that the combination of the ongoing response to the collapse of the Twin Towers and the threat of more terrorism made Lower Manhattan too dangerous for large numbers of civilians standing outside of their office buildings. In response to those concerns, New York City Mayor Rudy Giuliani ordered Lower Manhattan evacuated entirely.

Despite the evacuation order, evacuating millions of people who worked and lived in Lower Manhattan on any given weekday would not have been easy under normal circumstances, let alone 9/11. With the collapse of the Twin Towers, the PATH station that allowed New Jersey commuters to board trains back to New Jersey was destroyed. In addition, two Lower Manhattan subway stations were damaged by the collapse of the towers. Thus, neither the PATH nor the subway could help evacuate Lower Manhattan.

Moreover, motor vehicles could not use the closed bridges to leave the island. As a result, people who drove into the Lower Manhattan that morning were unable to drive out. Even if the bridges hadn't been closed, many people's cars were destroyed in the attacks or did not have their keys because the parking attendants who had them had already begun evacuating themselves.

Immediately after the dust cleared on the collapsed towers, first responders got into the debris to begin looking for survivors. In a span of minutes, the mission had switched from evacuation to rescue and recovery, setting off frantic searches across 16 acres of wreckage for survivors. The towers' collapse had also badly damaged all of the vehicles and equipment on site as well, and without any undamaged construction equipment available, first responders and volunteers were forced to remove debris by hand. The rescue effort was also hampered by concerns about the stability of surrounding buildings, and work was frequently stopped to ensure that no neighboring building was in danger of collapsing.

The name used for the area, Ground Zero, aptly described what rescue workers and reporters were seeing at the World Trade Center site after the towers collapsed. With the entire World Trade Center complex destroyed, the wreckage spread across several square acres. And despite Mayor Rudolph Giuliani's attempt to assure people that the air was safe to breathe, the enormous amount of dust that was released by the collapse of the towers made Ground Zero hard to even approach on September 11 and 12. For days afterward, the thick dust made breathing difficult in Lower Manhattan without a mask, and the collapse of the towers resulted in the largest release of asbestos in history, instantly leading to worries that people near the area would suffer respiratory problems.

The successful attacks, which destroyed the entire World Trade Center complex and killed about 3,000 people, were unlike anything the world had ever seen before, and it was carried out on a scale that had been unmatched by previous terrorist attacks with a plot that was practically undreamed of by Western intelligence. Just months before 9/11, convicted Oklahoma City bomber Timothy McVeigh had been executed, marking the demise of the man who had been responsible for the deadliest terrorist attack on American soil. McVeigh's attack had killed about 170 people, less than six percent of the casualties inflicted by al-Qaeda on 9/11. At the same time, Western intelligence was caught by surprise just as badly as the American public. Although a few FBI agents had theorized that terrorists were training in flight schools for the potential purpose of flying into targets, the intelligence community had continued to focus on preventing the kinds of attacks terrorists had been using for decades, such as car bombs and truck bombs, suicide attacks by individuals wearing bombs, and taking hostages for political ransom.

All 23 of the NYPD officers who perished in the attacks were posthumously presented with the 9/11 Heroes Medal of Valor, courtesy of President George W. Bush, and were separately honored with the New York City Police Department's Medal of Honor. The Critical Response Command division, which was established with a starting crew of 5,600 counter-terrorism specialists following 9/11, remains the department's "largest ad-hoc force."

Although the department was hailed for its heroic efforts on 9/11, less than 20 years later the NYPD remains at the center of various controversies, in particular its treatment of minorities. For years, residents had complained about the harassment of minorities and the shooting deaths of unarmed black men. According to the *Associated Press*, from 2000-2010, police brutality and misconduct settlements amounted to close to $1 billion. One officer was subject to seven lawsuits, all of which involved excessive use of force.

The advent of smartphones and viral videos have made it increasingly difficult for corrupt police officers and those who abuse their powers to hide their transgressions. In November 2011, two NYPD officers were caught on tape attacking 19-year-old Luis Solivan, and Solivan's subsequent complaint described the events leading up to the "sadistic assault": "The evening of November 14th...started out as a fairly ordinary one for...Solivan. That evening, he left his apartment on University Avenue in the Bronx, and walked to a local store, where he purchased cigarettes. He was unarmed, not engaged in any unlawful activity, and minding his own business." The officers, Solivan alleged, proceeded to follow him to his home and kicked down the front door without a warrant. When Solivan, as he claimed, rightfully resisted, the officers hosed him down with pepper spray and began to beat him. During the process, the officers supposedly slammed his head against the wall with such brute force that it bore a hole in his wall.

In 2012, just months after two other NYPD officers were filmed shooting the dog of a homeless man, the testimony of a former NYPD narcotics detective sent another round of shockwaves through the public. He had witnessed, on more than one occasion, his colleagues planting illicit substances on innocent minority suspects to help the department meet their arrest quotas. The controversial issue of the department's secret quota system has resurfaced in recent years, in part revived by the 2018 documentary *Crime + Punishment,* which followed a dozen black NYPD whistleblowers and their mission to demolish this unjust practice.

An untold number of Muslim New Yorkers have also been victimized by racism. A 2011 investigative series published by the *Associated Press* exposed a covert NYPD surveillance program that specifically targeted Muslims, as mosques, halal restaurants, and universities with large Muslim populations were all subject to scrutiny. Officers tapped the phones of Muslim students at more than 13 universities and downloaded their text messages, emails, and other electronic communications without reason or consent. The NYPD defended their actions, referring to the program as an unpleasant, but necessary and perfectly legal practice. The FBI, however, disagreed. Ronald Kessler of *The Daily News* noted, "What never came out is that the FBI considers the NYPD's intelligence gathering practices since 9/11 not only a waste of money, but a violation of Americans' rights. Said an FBI source: 'We will not be a party to it.'"

In response, the NYPD has taken steps in recent years to make amends. On June 6, 2019, nearly 50 years after the Stonewall Uprising, the department issued a public apology regarding the unwarranted violence the officers inflicted during the riots. "I do know what happened should not have happened," said Police Commissioner James O'Neill. "The actions taken by the NYPD were wrong – plain and simple. The actions and the laws were discriminatory and oppressive, and for that, I apologize."

Today, the New York Police Department reigns supreme as the largest police force in the United States. It can boast a total of 34,000 uniformed patrolmen and 51,000 overall employees, a ratio of 4.18 officers for every 1,000 New Yorkers. Its size surpasses even that of the FBI.

Online Resources

Other books about New York history by Charles River Editors

Other books about the NYPD on Amazon

Further Reading

Ackerman, S., Beckett, L., & Lartey, J. (2016, November 17). Rudy Giuliani: Divisive New York past has many in fear of Drumpf cabinet post. Retrieved July 18, 2019, from https://www.theguardian.com/us-news/2016/nov/17/rudy-giuliani-new-york-mayor-trump-cabinet

Andrew, S., & Ahmed, S. (2019, June 6). Fifty years after Stonewall, New York police apologize for the raid. Retrieved July 18, 2019, from https://edition.cnn.com/2019/06/06/us/stonewall-nypd-apology-trnd/index.html

Asbury, H. (1932, April 15). OLD HAYS. Retrieved July 18, 2019, from https://www.newyorker.com/magazine/1932/04/23/old-hays

Bagcal, J. (2016, June 28). The Top 10 Secrets of the NYC Police Department (NYPD). Retrieved July 18, 2019, from https://untappedcities.com/2016/06/28/the-top-10-secrets-of-the-nyc-police-department/10/

Bailey, W. G. (1995). *The Encyclopedia of Police Science*. Taylor & Francis.

Baker, K. (2015, May 18). 'Welcome to Fear City' – the inside story of New York's civil war, 40 years on. Retrieved July 18, 2019, from https://www.theguardian.com/cities/2015/may/18/welcome-to-fear-city-the-inside-story-of-new-yorks-civil-war-40-years-on

Bridenbaugh, C. (2013). *Cities in the Wilderness - The First Century of Urban Life in America 1625-1742*. Read Books.

Browne, A. (2015, June 11). A history of blacks in NYPD blue: It all started with Samuel Battle. Retrieved July 18, 2019, from https://www.nydailynews.com/opinion/arthur-browne-history-blacks-nypd-blue-article-1.2253916

Caldwell, M. (2005). *New York Night: The Mystique and Its History*. Simon and Schuster.

Chadwick, B. (2017, May 2). How Police Brutality Shaped New York City. Retrieved July 18, 2019, from http://www.thehistoryreader.com/modern-history/nypd_police_brutality/

Chadwick, B. (2017, April 26). New York's long history of police brutality: "Necessary force" goes all the way back to the beginning of the NYPD. Retrieved July 18, 2019, from https://www.salon.com/2017/04/25/new-yorks-long-history-of-police-brutality-necessary-force-goes-all-the-way-back-to-the-beginning-of-the-nypd/

Conlon, E. (2019, May 17). Old Hays and his Descendants: The Legacy of the Last High Constable of New York City. Retrieved July 18, 2019, from https://www1.nyc.gov/site/nypd/news/f0517/old-hays-his-descendants-legacy-the-last-high-constable-new-york-city#/0

Czitrom, D. (2016, June 28). The Origins of Corruption in the New York City Police Department. Retrieved July 18, 2019, from https://time.com/4384963/nypd-scandal-history/

Editors, A. C. (2015, August 12). "Rattle Watch" in 1658 National Law Enforcement Commemorative Silver Dollar Coin. Retrieved July 18, 2019, from http://atlcoin.com/atlcoinblog/2015/08/12/rattle-watch-in-1658-national-law-enforcement-commemorative-silver-dollar-coin/

Editors, A. T. (2015, August 11). How The Stonewall Riots Changed The Course Of History. Retrieved July 18, 2019, from https://allthatsinteresting.com/stonewall-riots

Editors, A. T. (2015, June 1). When Crack Was King: 1980s New York In Photos. Retrieved July 18, 2019, from https://allthatsinteresting.com/1980s-new-york

Editors, B. B. (2010, May 14). Case Files of the New York Police Department 1800-1915. Retrieved July 18, 2019, from http://www.boweryboyshistory.com/2010/05/case-files-of-new-york-police.html

Editors, C. B. (2019, May 13). Eric Garner's family cries as "I can't breathe" video is played in court. Retrieved July 18, 2019, from https://www.cbsnews.com/news/eric-garner-death-five-years-later-disciplinary-trial-launches-for-nypd-cop-accused-of-using-chokehold/

Editors, C. N. (2019, June). September 11 Terror Attacks Fast Facts. Retrieved July 18, 2019, from https://edition.cnn.com/2013/07/27/us/september-11-anniversary-fast-facts/index.html

Editors, E. N. (2013, October 24). The green lanterns outside city police precincts. Retrieved July 18, 2019, from https://ephemeralnewyork.wordpress.com/tag/rattle-watchmen-new-amsterdam/

Editors, H. C. (2010, February 9). New Amsterdam becomes New York. Retrieved July 18, 2019, from https://www.history.com/this-day-in-history/new-amsterdam-becomes-new-york

Editors, H. C. (2011). November 7, 1982: Port Authority Practices for Plane Crashing into the WTC. Retrieved July 18, 2019, from http://www.historycommons.org/entity.jsp?entity=new_york_city_police_department

Editors, H. N. (2015). Kingston Daily Freeman, Volume XLI, Number 277, 7 September 1912. Retrieved July 18, 2019, from https://news.hrvh.org/veridian/?a=d&d=kingstondaily19120907.2.21.14&srpos=0&

Editors, H. M. (2017). "Embryo Courtezans and Felons": New York Police Chief George W. Matsell Describes the City's Vagrant and Delinquent Children, 1849. Retrieved July 18, 2019, from http://historymatters.gmu.edu/d/6526/

Editors, H. C. (2017, May 31). Stonewall Riots. Retrieved July 18, 2019, from https://www.history.com/topics/gay-rights/the-stonewall-riots

Editors, I. A. (2010, August 12). The Beginnings of the NYPD. Retrieved July 18, 2019, from http://blog.insidetheapple.net/2010/08/beginnings-of-nypd.html

Editors, N. P. (2012, March 25). Teddy Roosevelt's 'Doomed' War On New York Vice. Retrieved July 18, 2019, from https://www.npr.org/2012/03/25/149000761/teddy-roosevelts-doomed-war-on-new-york-vice

Editors, N. H. (2016, December 11). "What's the Deal With:" Gleason's 1854 Illustration of the Police Uniforms & Fire-Style Helmets? Retrieved July 18, 2019, from http://nypdhistory.com/whats-the-deal-with-gleasons-1854-illustration-of-the-police-uniforms-adopted-included-fire-style-helmets/

Editors, N. Y. (2016, December 4). New York Exposed: The Lexow Committee. Retrieved July 18, 2019, from https://newyorkhistoryblog.org/2016/12/new-york-exposed-the-lexow-committee/

Editors, N. H. (2018, January 7). Historical Artifact! c. 1855 Frontispiece – The City of Brooklyn PD's First Chief of Police! Retrieved July 18, 2019, from http://nypdhistory.com/historical-artifact-c-1855-frontispiece-the-city-of-brooklyn-pds-first-chief-of-police/

Editors, N. H. (2018, August 26). What's the Deal with; the History & Lineage of the NYPD's 108th Precinct, Long Island City? Retrieved July 18, 2019, from http://nypdhistory.com/whats-the-deal-with-the-history-lineage-of-the-nypds-108th-precinct-long-island-city/

Editors, N. H. (2018, April 30). What's the Deal With; The Lineage of Jewish Police Chaplains in the NYPD? Retrieved July 18, 2019, from http://nypdhistory.com/whats-the-deal-with-the-lineage-of-jewish-police-chaplains-in-the-nypd/

Editors, N. H. (2018, April 21). What's the Deal with: The Present Rank Structure in the NYPD & The "Slaughter of 1907". Retrieved July 18, 2019, from http://nypdhistory.com/whats-the-deal-with-the-present-rank-structure-in-the-nypd-the-slaughter-of-1907/

Editors, O. D. (2017). New York City Police Department Fallen Officers. Retrieved July 18, 2019, from https://www.odmp.org/agency/2758-new-york-city-police-department-new-york

Editors, O. D. (2019). Fallen Officers from 9/11 Terrorist Attacks. Retrieved July 18, 2019, from https://www.odmp.org/search/incident/september-11-terrorist-attack

Editors, P. H. (2012, May 11). History of the New York City Police Department. Retrieved July 18, 2019, from http://purehistory.org/history-of-the-new-york-city-police-department/

Editors, P. O. (2012, March 12). Words to live by when you're out on patrol. Retrieved July 18, 2019, from https://www.policeone.com/patrol-issues/articles/5238923-Words-to-live-by-when-youre-out-on-patrol/

Editors, P. M. (2018). The History of Motorcycle Law Enforcement. Retrieved July 18, 2019, from http://www.policemotorunits.com/new-york-city--ny-police-department.html

Editors, S. R. (2005, December 30). RANK STRUCTURE OF THE METROPOLITAN POLICE. Retrieved July 18, 2019, from http://brooklynnorth.blogspot.com/2005_12_01_archive.html

Editors, S. W. (2012, January 17). NEW YORK'S IED TASK FORCE 1905-1919. Retrieved July 18, 2019, from https://www.standingwellback.com/new-yorks-ied-task-force-1905-1919/

Editors, S. D. (2015). Sacramento Daily Union, Volume 7, Number 141, 3 August 1878. Retrieved July 18, 2019, from https://cdnc.ucr.edu/cgi-bin/cdnc?a=d&d=SDU18780803.2.47&e=-------en--20--1--txt-txIN--------1

Editors, S. B. (2015). 10 Cool Different Variations of the Police Badge. Retrieved July 18, 2019, from http://blog.stationbay.com/different-variations-police-badge

Editors, T. M. (2016). Obituary: Death of George W. Matsell. Retrieved July 18, 2019, from https://timesmachine.nytimes.com/timesmachine/1877/07/26/89703314.pdf

Editors, T. P. (2018). HISTORY OF TRAFFIC. Retrieved July 18, 2019, from https://local1182.org/about-us/history-of-traffic/

Editors, U. S. (2010). New Amsterdam. Retrieved July 18, 2019, from https://www.u-s-history.com/pages/h4234.html

Editors, V. (2019, June 6). 50 years after Stonewall, the NYPD finally apologizes to the LGBTQ community. Retrieved July 18, 2019, from https://www.vox.com/2019/6/6/18655565/nypd-stonewall-apology

Editors, W. T. (2017, November 22). The New York City Police riot of 1857. Retrieved July 18, 2019, from https://windowthroughtime.wordpress.com/tag/the-metropolitan-and-municipal-police-forces-of-new-york/

Editors, W. (2019, May 6). History of the New York City Police Department. Retrieved July 18, 2019, from https://en.wikipedia.org/wiki/History_of_the_New_York_City_Police_Department

Ganeva, T. (2012, September 28). Nine terrifying facts about America's biggest police force. Retrieved July 18, 2019, from https://www.salon.com/2012/09/28/nine_terrifying_facts_about_americas_biggest_police_force/

Gershon, L. (2017, December 18). How Stereotypes of the Irish Evolved From 'Criminals' to Cops. Retrieved July 19, 2019, from https://www.history.com/news/how-stereotypes-of-the-irish-evolved-from-criminals-to-cops

Grisar, P. J. (2017). Meet High Constable Jacob Hays, New York's Forgotten Jewish Super Cop. Retrieved July 18, 2019, from https://forward.com/culture/425415/meet-high-constable-jacob-hays-new-yorks-forgotten-jewish-super-cop/

Guariglia, M. (2019, May 22). What the loss of the New York police museum means for criminal-justice reform. Retrieved July 18, 2019, from https://www.washingtonpost.com/outlook/2019/05/22/what-loss-new-york-police-museum-means-criminal-justice-reform/?utm_term=.e999629af384

Gunderman, D. (2016, November 27). A look at NYC Mayor Fernando Wood and the 1857 police riot — 'Blue versus blue as City Hall steps ran red'. Retrieved July 18, 2019, from https://www.nydailynews.com/news/national/nyc-mayor-fernando-wood-1857-police-riot-article-1.2883608

Harvey, I. (2017, February 2). The story of Theodore Roosevelt and the New York Police Department. Retrieved July 18, 2019, from https://www.thevintagenews.com/2017/02/02/the-story-of-theodore-roosevelt-and-the-new-york-police-department/

Hukle, G. W. (2014, July 7). Wooden Rattle from circa 1600 Image. Retrieved July 18, 2019, from https://www.authorgloriawaldronhukle.com/apps/photos/photo?photoid=193914058

Kaller, S. (2018). NYPD Commissioner Teddy Roosevelt Argues the Police Entrance Exam Keeps "Blockheads" Off the Force. Retrieved July 18, 2019, from https://www.sethkaller.com/item/1964-21122.99-NYPD-Commissioner-Teddy-Roosevelt-Argues-the-Police-Entrance-Exam-Keeps-"Blockheads"-Off-the-Force

Katersky, A. (2019, May 10). NYPD officers who died of 9/11-related illnesses in recent years added to memorial. Retrieved July 18, 2019, from https://abcnews.go.com/US/nypd-officers-died-911-related-illnesses-recent-years/story?id=62957647

Kennedy, R. C. (2001). On This Day: Harper's Weekly features a cartoon about William Devery. Retrieved July 18, 2019, from http://movies2.nytimes.com/learning/general/onthisday/harp/0906.html

Klasfeld, A. (2012, September 12). NYPD Abuse Caught|on Tape, Teen Says. Retrieved July 18, 2019, from https://www.courthousenews.com/nypd-abuse-caughton-tape-teen-says/

Klein, C. (2017, March 16). When America Despised the Irish: The 19th Century's Refugee Crisis. Retrieved July 18, 2019, from https://www.history.com/news/when-america-despised-the-irish-the-19th-centurys-refugee-crisis

Lockhart, P. R. (2019, June 7). Eric Garner died during a 2014 police encounter. An officer involved might lose his job. Retrieved July 18, 2019, from https://www.vox.com/identities/2019/5/17/18629673/eric-garner-daniel-pantaleo-trial-chokehold-nypd

Marton, J. (2015, June 16). Today in NYC History: The Police Riots of 1857. Retrieved July 18, 2019, from https://untappedcities.com/2015/06/16/today-in-nyc-history-the-police-riots-of-1857/

Mathias, C. (2012, May 15). NYPD Stop And Frisks: 15 Shocking Facts About A Controversial Program. Retrieved July 18, 2019, from https://www.huffpost.com/entry/nypd-stop-and-frisks-15-shocking-facts_n_1513362

Mathias, C., & Schwartz, C. (2014, July 18). The NYPD Has A Long History Of Killing Unarmed Black Men. Retrieved July 18, 2019, from https://www.huffpost.com/entry/killed-by-the-nypd-black-men_n_5600045

McCabe, S. (2012, August 11). Crime History: 'rattle watch' becomes original New World police force. Retrieved July 18, 2019, from https://www.washingtonexaminer.com/crime-history-rattle-watch-becomes-original-new-world-police-force

McNamara, R. (2019, June 19). Theodore Roosevelt and the New York Police Department. Retrieved July 18, 2019, from https://www.thoughtco.com/theodore-roosevelt-ny-police-department-1773515

Menton, F. (2016, May 18). The Devastation Of New York City's Economy. Retrieved July 18, 2019, from https://www.manhattancontrarian.com/blog/2016/5/18/the-devastation-of-new-york-citys-economy

Mustain, G. (2017, August 14). When the crack scourge swept New York City. Retrieved July 18, 2019, from https://www.nydailynews.com/new-york/crack-scourge-swept-new-york-city-article-1.813844

Nevins, J. (2018, August 23). 'We didn't ask permission': Behind an explosive NYPD documentary. Retrieved July 18, 2019, from https://www.theguardian.com/film/2018/aug/23/nypd-documentary-crime-and-punishment-stephen-maing

O'Sullivan, N. (2013, March 23). Scary tales of New York: Life in the Irish slums. Retrieved July 18, 2019, from https://www.irishtimes.com/culture/scary-tales-of-new-york-life-in-the-irish-slums-1.1335816

Ross, E. R. (2017, June 19). 5 Realities About The World's Scariest Police Department. Retrieved July 18, 2019, from https://www.cracked.com/article_24806_why-nypd-weirdest-police-department-in-world.html

Rossen, J. (2019, May 28). 8 Facts About the Stonewall Riots 50 Years Later. Retrieved July 18, 2019, from http://mentalfloss.com/article/583074/stonewall-riots-facts

Roth, M. P. (2018). *A History of Crime and the American Criminal Justice System*. Routledge.

Serena, K. (2017, September 21). The Story Behind The NYPD's Crazy-Corrupt 77th Precinct. Retrieved July 18, 2019, from https://allthatsinteresting.com/nypd-corruption

Taggart, K., & Hayes, M. (2018, April 16). Here's Why BuzzFeed News Is Publishing Thousands Of Secret NYPD Documents. Retrieved July 18, 2019, from https://www.buzzfeednews.com/article/kendalltaggart/nypd-police-misconduct-database-explainer

Whalen, B., & Doorey, D. (1998, March/April). The Birth of the NYPD. Retrieved July 18, 2019, from http://bjwhalen.com/article.htm

Free Books by Charles River Editors

We have brand new titles available for free most days of the week. To see which of our titles are currently free, click on this link.

Discounted Books by Charles River Editors

We have titles at a discount price of just 99 cents everyday. To see which of our titles are currently 99 cents, click on this link.

Printed in Great Britain
by Amazon